FAITH SEEKING FREEDOM
LIBERTARIAN CHRISTIAN
ANSWERS TO TOUGH QUESTIONS

DR. NORMAN HORN
DOUG STUART
KERRY BALDWIN
DICK CLARK

PRAISE FOR FAITH SEEKING FREEDOM

Faith Seeking Freedom is a basic primer on serious libertarianism seen through the informed intellects of serious Christians. Its Q&A format is easy to read, utterly faithful to Christian doctrine and libertarian beliefs, and leaves you fulfilled yet asking for more. I strongly recommend it.

Hon. Andrew P. Napolitano, Senior Judicial Analyst, Fox News Channel

"As a Christian libertarian, you get questions. A lot of questions. A lot of the same questions. Instead of stumbling for responses, why reinvent the wheel? Faith Seeking Freedom gives you the substantive and convincing answers you need in order to understand your own position more deeply and convey it to others."

Thomas E. Woods

Nothing true or worthwhile comes without skeptical inquiry, but a tough question doesn't always require a long-winded response. This latest contribution from the Libertarian Christian Institute proves that the best answers are often the concise ones, those that strike at the root of the matter while drawing from unassailable facts and the ripest wisdom.

Lawrence W. Reed, president emeritus of the Foundation for Economic Education and author of Was Jesus a Socialist?

In Faith Seeking Freedom, the authors draw on Judeo-Christian principles to provide a helpful and accessible guide to the ideas and public policies of a free society. For both modern Christians and secularists alike, this book offers insights into how to steer through the cultural seductions and dangers of tyranny to reach the greater human well-being only made possible through liberty.

David J. Theroux, Founder and President, Independent Institute; Founder and President, C.S. Lewis Society of California

"It's tough to imagine any Christian reading this book and not embracing the non-aggression principle of libertarianism."

Mary Ruwart, Chair, Liberty International

We all have an almost endless number of questions, especially when it comes to an issue as complex as the relationship between government and our Christian faith. Answers – now those are much harder to come by. Faith Seeking Freedom is a good place to start. It offers some solid answers to those questions – over 100 of them! The Q&A format makes for easy reading but don't let the brevity of the answers fool you. They pack an intellectual punch presented with sound reason and plenty of scriptural support. And the authors put "tough questions" in the title for a reason. They don't skirt the most difficult issues. In fact, they take them head-on. Whether you're a long-time libertarian Christian seeking to better defend your position or a curious bystander trying to figure it all out, this book is a must-read.

Mike Maharrey, Host of the GodArchy Podcast

A very useful contribution that strikes a good balance between comprehensive answers and a wide variety of issues. The questions are indeed the tough ones that would come from Christians who do not embrace libertarianism; honest readers will appreciate the sincere attempts to meet these objections.

Robert P. Murphy, Senior Fellow, Mises Institute

Faith Seeking Freedom is wonderfully clear, concise, and kind to the reader. This book will help non-libertarian Christians to better understand, respect, and maybe even adopt libertarianism as their favored approach to political philosophy.

Kevin Vallier, Associate Professor of Philosophy, Bowling Green State University

Faith Seeking Freedom is an excellent and useful collection of handy answers to important questions. Is it filled with conversation-enders? No—it's filled with conversation starters, and that's what makes it important.

Art Carden, Professor of Economics and Medical Properties Trust Fellow, Brock School of Business, Samford University

You can find a fair amount of Christian libertarian theory online today, and in no small contribution from the authors that have collaborated here, but there are few options for comprehensive reading. Narrowing our options even further, would be the expressed desire for something thoroughly covering the breadth of Christian libertarian philosophy, while remaining accessible for the beginner and worthwhile for the familiar. Faith Seeking Freedom is an achieving apologetic. This catechism quickly surveys the vast subject, while responsibly addressing necessary distinctions in existing political theories that reside under the often umbrella terms of 'Christian,' and 'libertarian.' I am thankful for the authoring and editing efforts that went into the creation of this book. It can easily serve to clarify terms, and offer consistency, to formed or forming convictions, where our faith dictates our politics.

Stephen Rose, AnarchoChristian.com

I must confess that I am not fond of the term "libertarianism" for the same reason I find "capitalism" misleading. In almost any debate over libertarianism, one must spend half the time explaining what it is not before moving on to what it might be. If libertarianism means libertinism, count me out. As pointed out in this text however, libertarianism is not a full-fledged philosophy, much less a theology, as much as it is an argument that maintains (in Lord Acton's words) that "liberty is the political end of man," – not, of course, his entire telos.

This book is not the final word on the argument between the Christian revelation and human liberty, but it nonetheless asks many of the right questions, questions that are rarely raised among Christians.

Rev. Robert A. Sirico, Acton Institute

Achieving liberty will require enlightening our fellow men about its eternal truths. The contributors to this volume, Christians who are also principled and articulate libertarians, argue for a more libertarian interpretation of Christian teachings, and seek to explain to fellow Christians and other people of faith the glory and morality of liberty in terms they will already relate to. Liberty is ultimately about peace, love, and cooperation, which is a message that can appeal to the 2.4 billion Christians on the planet. This is a big potential audience. This is an important book and undertaking.

Stephan Kinsella

I am delighted, exhilarated, and deliriously pleased with the publication of this book. It is an excellent attempt to convince Christians, the co-creators of Western Civilization, to adopt libertarian principles. I can attest that the authors are well-steeped in libertarian theory. If anyone can make the case for the freedom philosophy to Christians, it is this team from the Libertarian Christian Institute.

— *Walter Block, Senior Fellow, Mises Institute*

"As a Jewish agnostic who is also a libertarian, I found this book to be absorbing and persuasive. I can recommend it wholeheartedly to other Jewish agnostics, whether or not they're libertarian. On that basis, it looks like a must-read for folks of the Christian faith!"

—*Gene Epstein, Director of The Soho Forum*

Faith Seeking Freedom: Libertarian Christian Answers to Tough Questions

Libertarian Christian Institute Press
www.libertarianchristians.com

ISBN: 978-1-7336584-4-7

CONTENTS

4 DOES A FREE SOCIETY HAVE LIMITS?   42

5 IS CAPITALISM PROBLEMATIC?   48

6 WHAT ABOUT CHRISTIAN MORALS AND ETHICS?   55

7 WHAT ABOUT PUBLIC GOODS AND SERVICES? 64

8 WHAT ABOUT NATIONALISM, NATION STATE, & PATRIOTISM? 73

9 WHAT ABOUT SOCIAL JUSTICE? 78

10 WHAT ABOUT IMMIGRATION? 83

11 WHAT ABOUT ABORTION? 91

12 WHAT ABOUT THE ENVIRONMENT & CREATION?   104

13 CHRISTIAN MISCONCEPTIONS OF LIBERTARIANISM   110

To our friends who weren't afraid
to ask us tough questions on important issues.
And to the author of liberty, Soli Deo Gloria.

FAITH SEEKING FREEDOM
LIBERTARIAN CHRISTIAN
ANSWERS TO TOUGH QUESTIONS

FOREWORD

"I would have written a shorter letter," the French theologian Blaise Pascal once declared, "but I didn't have the time."

Pascal's meaning was profound. To make a point, we have two length-related options. We can write on and on, tossing in every thought big or small, and hope readers will read it. Or we can be pithy and concise enough that no reader will have a good reason not to, a talent that poor writers envy. It's that course for which the authors of Faith Seeking Freedom have opted. The result is a one-stop shop of powerful and penetrating responses to more than a hundred excellent questions.

This is a book that addresses both Christianity and libertarianism, the political philosophy of liberty. In my teen years more than half a century ago, I was increasingly drawn to both but puzzled that they sometimes seemed at odds. However, the more I learned about Christianity and libertarianism, the more I came to understand their indissoluble compatibility. I even wrote a book titled Was Jesus a Socialist? that presented that case. Now, with this volume from the Libertarian Christian Institute, no one hereafter can ever make a convincing argument that the teachings of Christ and the principles of liberty are incongruous.

Liberty is an environment in which everyone makes choices about their life without fearing the initiation of force against them. In other words, liberty means you get to be the unique individual God intended you to be, so long as you do not threaten others. The Creator did not make us mindless robots to be programmed by some privileged central planner. The better we understand what liberty is, especially its insistence on strong moral character, the more it is obvious that it comports perfectly with the ethics of Christianity. Both libertarianism and the teachings of Christ demand that we respect one another, do no harm to each other, assist our fellows in distress, celebrate free will and diversity, and interact in peace.

It is a good thing to wonder and to raise questions. Even the Apostle Thomas had his doubts. There was a time, for example, when I was stumped over the matter of Jesus driving the so-called moneychangers from the Temple. A college professor told us it was an indication that Jesus had a problem with people who were trying to make money, that he was anti-market or anti-wealth. Why else would he do such a thing, I asked myself?

Later upon reflection, I realized that Jesus never drove a moneychanger from a bank or a marketplace. What seemed like a tough issue for a libertarian could be answered in a sentence or two. God's house simply was a uniquely holy and inappropriate place for what the moneychangers were doing.

The story of Jesus feeding some 5,000 people, as told in the books of Matthew and John, is well known throughout the world. It goes like this:

> As a large and hungry crowd gathers to hear Jesus, his disciples nervously ask him how so many people can be fed. The only food in their midst consists of five loaves of bread and two fishes. Jesus informs his associates of some rich people who live nearby. "Go and take what they have and give it to these who want it" he commands.
>
> So armed with swords and clubs the disciples raid the homes of the rich, as well as a grocery store and a bank, and redistribute the proceeds to the grateful multitude. After the event is over, Jesus lobbies Roman authorities to

raise taxes on the rich and fork over the loot so that next time the disciples will not have to go steal it themselves.

Of course, that is not the real story at all. Jesus never commanded anyone to swipe somebody else's property, not even for a "good cause." In this instance, he solved the problem not by pilfering other people's pockets, but by the power of the Holy Spirit to create new wealth. However, I know there are many Christians out there who believe that this story of feeding the multitude shows that Jesus was sympathetic to a generous welfare state. They are usually the same folks who think the generous traveler in the Good Samaritan story was a socialist, even though he solved the stricken man's problem with private charity, not public handouts.

Reasonable questions, brief but pointed answers. That is the formula that makes this book work. And the authors never suggest that their responses are everything that can be said about an issue. Great recommendations for further reading are provided in several places.

If you are already a libertarian Christian, you will still find this book to be of great value and loaded with insights you may not have previously considered. If you are new to either Christianity or to libertarianism, you will find gems on every page. This is a keeper, a book you will want to keep handy on your most prominent bookshelf and one that you will recommend to others repeatedly.

I could go on and on, but not without proving Pascal's wisdom at my own expense. Read this book with an open mind and you will be amazed at the extent to which its authors will fill it.

Lawrence W. Reed
President Emeritus and Humphreys
Family Senior Fellow
Foundation for Economic Education
Atlanta, Georgia
September 2020

INTRODUCTION

The human heart has a natural orientation toward liberty. We are built this way, regardless of our religion or ethnicity; indeed, all men are endowed with liberty and a deep desire for it.

— Rev. Robert A. Sirico

Despite the accelerating rate of innovation and progress humans have made in recent centuries, we have yet to defeat our inner desire to conquer and dominate one another. Read the latest newspaper headline, watch half a news segment, or scroll for five seconds through a social media feed, and you will find ample evidence of the human yearning to control the lives of others. From your acquaintances on social media to the highest offices in the country, the yearning for power is evident. Lawmakers enact policies that manipulate the economic playing field to favor themselves or their friends. Law enforcement agents zealously use overwhelming force to stop minor infractions. Governors promise citizens that if they would just obey orders, their problems will soon be healed. To see these emerging social patterns takes stepping back and critically assessing what's happening, but it is visible to all who care to see it.

To make matters even more complicated, the corporate press and competing institutions exacerbate our social conflicts by weaving narratives that leave us tangled in confusion. We are inundated with demands to take a side and stake our claim to power, or else be canceled for not standing up for what the other side says is right. Standing up for truth has become all about rising up to grasp power.

Christians in America have also fallen prey to this phenomenon, seeking status, privilege, and power from an institution that the Church has historically viewed with suspicion. It is as though we have forgotten Jesus' words to his disciples in Matthew 20: "You know that the rulers of the Gentiles lord it over them, and their great ones are tyrants over them. It will not be so among you; but whoever wishes to be great among you must be your servant, and whoever wishes to be first among you must be your slave." Even the American founding myth of distrust of the state has been abandoned for the pursuit of absolute power and dominance. Both Christians and non-Christians have become re-enchanted by the allure of empire. The days when it was patriotic to question your government seem like a bygone era. Worse yet, many Christians have lost the ability to think straightforwardly about the world without importing an agenda driven by the desire for political power. As Brian Zahnd says repeatedly, the world is "addicted to solving its problems through violence," but the cross "demands that we renounce violence as a means of achieving just ends." A truly Christian political philosophy includes embracing just means toward just ends, and violence is never the answer.

This lost habit of thinking about politics in a Christian way must be recovered. The biblical prophets preached against the evils of empire, and the Messiah declared his supremacy over the kingdoms of this world. Today, Christians need to model those examples and herald the good news that speaks truth to power.

This prophetic voice against empire should incline us, as Christians, toward promoting individual liberty, free markets, and non-aggression. Empire wants to subsume our human agency, robbing each of us of our dignity as image-bearers of God. We wrote this book because we believe the growing threat of empire is a battle worth fighting, and we fight against it by arming ourselves with clear, compelling, and (when possible) concise answers to tough questions.

To be clear, we wage battle not by wielding any kind of physical violence or threats of violence, but with words. As the Apostle Paul wrote, our struggle "is not against enemies of blood and flesh, but against the rulers, against the authorities, against the cosmic powers of this present darkness, against the spiritual forces of evil in the heavenly places" (Eph. 6:12). Our fight is not with *people* but with *ideas*, and so we must endeavor to "destroy arguments and every proud obstacle raised up against the knowledge of god, and we take every thought captive to obey Christ" (2 Cor. 10:4-5).

In any battle, a strong defense is necessary to win. We take seriously what Peter wrote in 1 Peter 3:15: "Always be ready to make your defense to anyone who demands from you an accounting for the hope that is in you." It is in Jesus Christ (not worldly powers such as the state) we find our hope. It is to Christ, not Caesar, we pledge our allegiance.

In the past decade or so, many Christians have affirmed what we believe about libertarianism: it is the modern political philosophy most consistent with the Christian faith. If you count yourself among us libertarian Christians (or close to it), we hope that this book will arm you with strong answers to questions. This is not a light endeavor. Convincing others that your political beliefs are the best way to think about the world is always challenging. Very rarely are people convinced by the mere articulation of a viewpoint. Objections must be dealt with and questions must be answered. Sometimes those answers are not wholly satisfying, but are enough to keep one searching and seeking. And if you are the one who is asked the questions, you want to be equipped with clear, concise answers that are convincing enough to move the conversation forward.

A word of caution is necessary, as well. While the battle of ideas rages on, we must always remember we are conversing with human beings whose minds can be changed. Being equipped with solid answers will help, but answers alone are not the solution. Our approach must always be seasoned with empathy, love, and respect for those who ask us questions. We must learn from their questions, both to understand their side better and to sharpen our answers for them. So while we wrote this book to help readers deal with an important aspect of the conversation, it is up to them to listen and respond in grace and with respect.

The purpose of this book is two-fold. If you are a libertarian Christian, we hope this book equips you with solid responses to the common objections so you can be better equipped to make the Christian case for a free society. If you are a non-libertarian seeking answers to the tough questions about politics, we hope this book will get you started on a journey that leads you to a greater understanding of the libertarian Christian perspective, and perhaps even convinces you to join us!

We want this book to be as clear and concise as possible while also being conversational in tone. The questions are grouped together into chapters topically, and those topics have been organized to represent a basic flow of a conversation. We recommend reading from beginning to end, but readers who choose to jump around will not lose much, if anything.

Each chapter ends with "Further Reading," a curated list of books, articles, and other resources to learn more about the topics within that chapter. Of course, we do not endorse everything said by every author, but they provide a solid range of libertarian and Christian works, some of which have been highly regarded for many decades. You can also view the full reading list by visiting www.faithseekingfreedom.com, where we will add more resources even after the printing of this book.

Each contributor to this book has their own set of beliefs and opinions about politics and theology while also adhering to the historic Christian faith as proclaimed since the first century. Libertarian thought exists on a spectrum, and so the authors will answer these questions from varying places along that spectrum. However, we all agree on the fundamental aspects of the libertarian creed and the broad outlines of what a free society looks like. Of course, like most libertarians, we enjoy arguing together over the particulars. What is important for the purposes of this book is that we all advocate for consistent application of individual liberty in every possible circumstance.

Lastly, we must note that, while we spend a great deal of energy defending a free society from a Christian perspective, none of these authors believe that libertarianism is the ultimate hope for our world. We firmly believe a free society with peaceful exchange is best, but the ultimate hope for humanity comes only from God through the saving work of Jesus Christ. Let us never forget that, "Salvation belongs to our God who is seated on the throne, and to the Lamb" (Rev. 7:10). To God be the glory, as we seek to honor him even in our political ideas.

1

WHY SHOULD I CARE ABOUT POLITICS?

"The fact that the problem of Church and State is of such central importance is a corollary of the [end times] attitude of Christianity. Because the Gospel presents itself as the 'politeuma,' the community of the coming age, it must accordingly see as its most intrinsic concern its disposition toward the present 'polis,' the secular State, and therefore not [uncritically accept it] - as if the State itself were something final, definitive."

— Oscar Cullmann

1. Politics isn't a gospel issue, so why should I be concerned about politics?

Most people think of politics as *electoral* politics: elections, politicians, and voting. A more robust understanding is that politics is more like a subset of the ways in which human beings choose to relate, specifically with regard to the appropriate use of physical force and power.

"Culture" is another means of how we relate to each other, and while part of that is political, much of it is not. In this sense, the saying "politics is life" is true. When we advocate anything that affects the lives of others, we are doing politics in this very broad sense. Most Christians believe that the gospel has implications for the real world, which makes the gospel relevant to politics. This also means that Christians are political, whether they realize it or not.

Libertarian Christians care about how people in the world relate to one another in ways that align with the ethic and message of the Kingdom of God. We do not say that all Christians should vote for a particular type of candidate, or even vote at all. Not only do we want Christians to be aware of the human relationships that are part of what it means to be human, but also at the forefront of pushing human relationships toward mutual benefit and interacting peacefully (see Chapters 3-4).

2. Jesus said his Kingdom was not of this world. Isn't political engagement being concerned with "this world"?

As Jesus announced the coming of God's Kingdom, throughout the Gospels we see that his Kingdom did not operate upon the principles of worldly kingdoms ("not of this world"). This doesn't mean that the Kingdom of God is not for this world. The very word "kingdom" is inherently political, meaning "the king's domain."

Modern Christians often miss the explicitly political language of the New Testament. The phrases "Jesus is Lord" and "Son of God" were, in Jesus' day, an affront to Caesar. It was Caesar who rode into cities on a war horse demanding people's allegiance, promising an age of peace won by violence, and demanding submission. In contrast, Jesus came promising the life of the age to come ("eternal life") through faith in him, a peace that was not won through violence, but through the forgiveness of sins and allegiance to him.

To give allegiance to Jesus Christ is to strip Rome of its power and authority. This is how the gospel is a direct challenge to the state and to its power. In part, when Christians invite others to believe the gospel, they are inviting them to declare allegiance to God, not the state.

3. Politics just seems like a distraction from the real mission of the Church.

When a person gives their life to Jesus Christ, they are also giving their allegiance to a new king. Today this often does not amount to defying the current political regimes, but it does mean a new way of thinking, practicing, and evangelizing. Instead of allegiance to mammon, we preach allegiance to God. Instead of pursuit of pleasure for its own sake, we seek to enjoy all things to the glory of God. We honor the one true king when we promote the good news that Jesus is the messiah and through him we can have eternal life (which, by definition, begins before death).

To repent and believe the good news entails far more than what happens to us personally. It is not simply for us to have a private religious experience. Jesus inaugurated a Kingdom over which his rule would be established through what would become his followers: the body of Christ, or the Church. Kingdom people are his royal subjects, working to bring the whole creation to bear witness to the good news that Jesus is Lord, and Caesar is not.

To be engaged in spreading the gospel is to announce the arrival of God's Kingdom, followed by an invitation to repent and participate in this Kingdom. Participation happens in a variety of ways, some of which look more "political" than others. But every one of our efforts are political in the sense that we are engaging the world around us in ways that bring about more flourishing, even if these efforts are not directly engaged in electoral politics.

4. So what does God have to say about government?

God does speak about governance in scripture, and there has been much debate about the implications of what he says. Inferred by this is usually a question of whether a particular political philosophy is prescribed by God. In other words, would Jesus have been a socialist? A Republican? Alternatively, there is a popular view that Christians must submit to government regardless of the lawlessness of its edicts. We disagree.

Scripture speaks to the fact of civil governance and its necessity (Rom. 13:1-7; 1 Pet. 2:13-14; Titus 3:1), but it does not explicate a precise way of administering civil governance. In other words, God doesn't give us an operations manual for providing the service of civil justice. What God provides are norms of civil justice that are evident in creation and are therefore comprehensible by all human beings. However, the systems by which humanity has administered (or attempted to administer) civil justice are human inventions known as political philosophies.

Political philosophies are attempts to articulate the best way of achieving a just system of governance. Libertarianism is one such philosophy, and we believe it's the best expression of Christian political thought because it most aligns with God-given norms expressed in scripture and evidenced in nature.

One important distinction we make is between "the state" and "civil governance," and in our view the state is inherently bad and tends to corrupt good civil governance. As Christians, we can take our cue from historic Christian orthodoxy and the historic confessions of faith. These only oblige Christian submission to civil authorities on matters that are lawful ordinances of God. But they don't obligate abject submission to all edicts and don't oppose resistance to unlawful or unrestrained sword power. Because of this, we hold the distinction between "the state" and "civil governance" to be legitimate and necessary.

5. Didn't Paul write that governments were established by God?

Romans 13:1 does say that the authorities that exist are "established by God," but Romans 13 is definitely not a prooftext for justifying state power.

True, Paul proceeds to caution against rebellion and encourage doing "what is right" in the eyes of the ruler to protect oneself.

But these words were written to Christians in Rome who were constantly at risk of persecution, even unto death, from the Roman Empire. Paul's encouragement to them, and likewise to us, is that our interactions with state power are on a prudential basis. Our greater priorities are to live out the gospel and support our family and community, and we should not put ourselves into a compromising position against the state unless it is specifically for the cause of Christ and his message.

Therefore, we pay our taxes not because the government has a divine right to tax us, but rather because if we don't, we might end up in prison and unable to fulfill our true calling to protect our families and spread the gospel. Ultimately, we should also turn to other scriptures to get a full view of what the Bible has to say about the state instead of only reading Romans 13 and thinking that we fully understand God's intention for government.

6. What scriptural support is there that the state is inherently bad?

Amazingly enough, it all begins in the book of Genesis. The Tower of Babel narrative (Genesis 11) is the "origin story" of the state. In the passage, we learn that the people of Babel aspire to build for themselves a tower that would "reach the heavens" so that they could "make for themselves a name." They do this as they "journey eastward," which parallels the language of separation from God being "east of Eden."

Many commentators as far back as the first-century Jewish historian Josephus have noted that these things together mean they are either literally or symbolically rebelling against God by trying to take over heaven itself. They are responding to their separation not by turning to God in repentance but by turning *against* God entirely.

In Jewish antiquities writing, it was Nimrod, the "mighty rebel" before the Lord (some versions read "hunter," but this is not the best translation) and the first king of Babel/Babylon, who incited them to do so. God disrupts their plan and scatters them about both in their location and in their languages. We can see this story as the theological beginning of all states, which are ultimately founded in rebellion against God and trying to take the place of God on the earth.

7. But didn't the Israelites have kings? Doesn't that mean having a state is okay?

It is true that the Israelites had kings, but do not forget that God brought them out of Egypt so that he alone could be their king. Their request for a human king as recorded in 1 Samuel 8 is granted, but not without a stern and prescient warning for what the government they asked for would ultimately do to them:

> These will be the ways of the king who will reign over you: he will take your sons and appoint them to his chariots and to be his horsemen, and to run before his chariots… He will take your daughters… He will take the best of your fields and vineyards… and you shall be his slaves. And in that day you will cry out because of your king, whom you have chosen for yourselves; but the LORD will not answer you in that day. (1 Sam. 8:11-18)

This is an incredible statement! God says that because they are choosing a human king rather than God as their king, they will be set upon by the human government they have chosen. Their sons will be sent to war (conscription), the human king will take their land and possessions (taxation), and they will literally be made to be his slaves.

So much for the supposed virtue of the democratic process! Though God worked through Israelite kings to accomplish his ultimate plan, that was never God's preference from the beginning.

8. If the Old Testament is not favorable toward government, what about the New Testament?

A major theme of the New Testament is the contrast between the Kingdom of God and the "Kingdoms of this world." Jesus says one seeks to dominate and the other to serve (Matt. 20:25). Which do you think Jesus wants us aligned with?

More importantly, Jesus' temptations in the desert give us a special insight into the nature and allure of state power. We read in Matthew 4 that Satan offered Jesus the Kingdoms of the world if only Jesus would bow down and worship Satan. Did Jesus respond with "What do you mean? They don't belong to you; you couldn't give them to me if you tried!" Nope. If that were the case, it wouldn't have been a temptation at all. Instead, Jesus gives tacit recognition that Satan could do what he offered, and retorts with "worship the Lord your God and serve only him" (Matt. 4:10). The message to us, evidently, is that the state is inherently on board with Satan, not God.

Interestingly, Paul says in Ephesians 6:12 that our struggle is "not against flesh and blood" but against "the rulers, against the authorities, against the cosmic powers of this present darkness, against the spiritual forces of evil in the heavenly places." Even if we take that list as being primarily spiritual, we must still try to understand how Paul could say this while knowing that the Roman government was oppressing so many, especially Christians. We then realize that Christians can show godly love toward those in government positions while still seeing their power as evil.

9. Government rule, then, might not be the right way to go. What hope do we have against powerful states?

Glad you asked, because God has a plan for the state and its machinations, and we get to join into his plan through Jesus and his church. Of course, we have hope in the gospel message itself that brings salvation both right now and in the future. We have the Holy Spirit that indwells us right now and sanctifies us throughout our life. We have the ability to make a difference right now, and we have the great hope of final victory in the end. After all, as the book of Revelation shows us, we know that the final destination of these "powers that be" is destruction.

Remember all that weird language around "Babylon" in Revelation? We hear about the fall of it as a city, and it is even personified in three ways in the book: as the dragon, as the "beast out of the sea," and even as the "Mother of Prostitutes and Abominations." (Gross!) Theologians have debated how to interpret the Revelation to John for centuries, but the attentive reader can see in "Babylon" both the Roman Empire of John's day and the symbolic connection to Babel from Genesis. The symbol is a culmination and representation of statism—of violent, aggressive power—for all time.

God assures us that no matter what, Jesus has won the victory against all sin, all death, and all competing powers. Even the first time Babylon is specifically mentioned in Revelation, it is when an angel declares, "Fallen, fallen is Babylon the Great!" (Rev. 14:8) In the end, God wins.

10. Does being a libertarian mean joining a political party?

Plato and Aristotle described the existence of political factions in classical Athens, and this dynamic is still characteristic of politics today. Modern political parties as we know them first began emerging in the 18th and 19th centuries. These parties sprang from political ideologies and existing—often pragmatic—political coalitions. In some countries, third parties play a substantial role in government. However, in the United States, there are two dominant political parties, and third parties are limited by ballot access rules, debate participation, and other constraints that drastically limit both their success in electoral politics and their ability to effect change in government.

Libertarianism is a theory of justice, not a political party affiliation. Some libertarians choose to become active in the Libertarian Party or another political party in order to try to influence elections or to have the opportunity to share libertarian ideas in a public forum. Other libertarians prefer to avoid electoral politics altogether. The formation of the Libertarian Party of the United States in 1971 was opposed by some prominent libertarians. The Libertarian Party remains controversial among libertarians today. Christians should be led by their convictions and prayerful reflection on the best ways to help build God's Kingdom and regenerate goodness into society's structure.

Further Reading

"New Testament Theology of the State, Part 1 and Part 2" | Norman Horn (Libertarian Christian Institute, 2008)

Bible and Government: Public Policy from a Christian Perspective | John Cobin (Alertness Books, 2003)

Christian Theology of Public Policy: Highlighting the American Experience | John Cobin (Alertness Books, 2006)

Resisting Babel: Allegiance to God and the Problem of Government | John Mark Hicks, ed. (Abilene Christian University Press, 2020)

"Jesus Wasn't a Libertarian (but He's Glad I Am!)" | Doug Stuart (Libertarian Christian Institute, 2018)

Kingdom Conspiracy: Returning to the Radical Mission of the Local Church | Scot McKnight (Brazos Press, 2014)

The State in the New Testament | Oscar Cullmann (Charles Scribner's Sons, 1956)

2

THE LIBERTARIAN BASICS

"Consider the roads blocked up by robbers, the seas beset with pirates, wars scattered all over the earth with the bloody horror of camps. The whole world is wet with mutual blood; and murder, which in the case of an individual is admitted to be a crime, is called a virtue when it is committed wholesale. Impunity is claimed for the wicked deeds, not on the plea that they are guiltless, but because the cruelty is perpetrated on a grand scale."

- St. Cyprian, 250 AD

11. What makes somebody a libertarian?

Liberty means being free to live your life as your conscience leads you. A libertarian is a person who generally opposes forcible compulsion of peaceful people. The central, defining tenet of libertarianism is often referred to as the "non-aggression principle" (NAP). According to the NAP, no person should initiate violence against a non-aggressor.

Libertarians love peaceful, voluntary cooperation with others. Libertarians categorically reject actions that violate the rights of others to their own lives, liberty, and property. Libertarians believe that peace is both ethically preferable to violence and better for making society prosperous. However, the NAP differs from radical pacifism in an important way: it allows for the use of proportional force in retaliation against an aggressor (a person who violates the rights of another person). NAP also differs from the harm principle in that the focus is on the action initiated, rather than the harm caused.

Libertarians do not believe in using physical force to prevent people from indulging in vices or to punish them for their bad habits. This is because libertarians do not believe the use of force is justified when a person's action does not violate the rights of others. Most libertarians still regard harmful vices as wasteful, undesirable, and even immoral. Libertarian Christians generally maintain the traditional, biblical view on being wise and fleeing from sinful indulgence (2 Tim. 2:22). We deny that force and compulsion are the best means for addressing such sinful behavior and its earthly and eternal consequences.

12. How is the non-aggression principle (NAP) consistent with a Christian worldview?

The NAP is premised on the idea that people have individual rights, including the right to their own bodies and the right to their physical property. As Christians, we believe that God made man in his image. Living peaceably with other people (Rom. 12:18; Mark 9:50) and treating them as we want to be treated is a thoroughly Christian idea that is specifically and repeatedly commanded in the Bible (Luke 6:31, Gal. 5:14).

Refraining from murder (Gen. 4:10–11), kidnapping (Ex. 21:16), assault (Ex. 21:18), theft (Matt. 19:18), fraud (Prov. 20:23), and other offenses against others is, of course, all in accord with the counsel of scripture. The legal principles set out by God for Israel included detailed protection for property rights and prescriptions for legal remedies (e.g., Ex. 22:1–9).

Christians are called to be respectful to everyone, including those who temporarily occupy positions of social authority (1 Pet. 2:17). But we should not be swayed by popularity and worldly rank when we are analyzing questions of right and wrong (Rom. 2:11–12). A Christian theory of justice applies equally to all people, including elected officials and people employed by government bureaucracies (see Question 28).

The NAP is not a comprehensive guide to righteous living. It is merely a principle of justice—a rule about when force may be employed as a solution. Its answer is clear: violence is justified only in response to aggression against people and their property.

13. How do libertarian Christians account for people who violate the non-aggression principle (NAP)?

Violations of the NAP constitute crimes. More precisely, they are rights violations. The proper role of civil governance is to administer justice when rights violations occur. Libertarians know these violations are just a fact of life. Christians know these violations occur as a result of the sinful nature of man. So what do we do when these violations occur?

Holding people accountable for rights violations is in many ways not too different from the system we have. The problem with the current system is its propensity to corruption, malfeasance, and an inability of the state to be impartial in its own case. But many of the principles we're already familiar with, such as presumption of innocence, proof beyond a reasonable doubt, and a fair and speedy trial, would still be present in a libertarian system. The punitive system would likely differ; restitution for rights violations would be preferable to prison sentences in many cases. Things such as mandatory minimums, solitary confinement, and special interests jockeying for preferential treatment from the state, wouldn't likely exist.

A libertarian minarchist society would be a decentralized version of what we have now, while a libertarian anarchist society would be some polycentric iteration which employs these principles. The colloquial use of the term 'anarchy' implies a sense of chaos and lawlessness, and Christians are indeed morally obligated to reject chaos and lawlessness. However, this common usage isn't accurate. The etymology of the term simply means *without rulers*. The colloquial use implies that, without rulers we would have chaos and lawlessness.

Libertarian anarchists don't agree. Rather, they hold that chaos and lawlessness is produced through a monopoly on civil governance, since the state's very existence depends on violations of the NAP, namely theft (through taxation) and violence (through a monopoly use of legal force). In either a libertarian minarchist or anarchist society violations of the NAP can be handled in a just manner.

14. Why are property rights so important to libertarians?

Christians believe that all things are ultimately owned by God in Christ (Col. 1:15-17). Humans, as image bearers of God, are given stewardship over themselves and their property. This stewardship is not only a responsibility we have to God, but it is a right we have in relation to each other.

Human rights are foundational in a libertarian society due to their normativity. In the words of Frederic Bastiat, "[rights] do not exist because men have made laws. On the contrary, it was the fact that [rights] existed beforehand that caused men to make laws in the first place." But how do we identify or articulate them? This has been the problem philosophers have faced for centuries, even back to ancient times. Property rights, however, are a useful way to clearly identify human rights. Christians may claim property rights (in their person and of their things) vis-à-vis Christ's teaching in Matthew 20 (see especially verse 15) and Luke's reference in Acts 5:4.

In fact, property rights are so useful that Murray Rothbard said they're axiomatic; that is, self-evidently true. Christians can agree stating this is a God-given norm through creation, which is why they are self-evident. Because property rights are evidenced by nature, human beings (whether believers or not) may operate on the same rules, and we don't need to teach every individual a contrived political-economic theory.

Property rights are useful because everyone recognizes them regardless of their personal political proclivities. Even socialists believe in property rights; they simply believe the government has the right to a given property. So libertarians operate from a principle of property rights because they are universally understood and self-evident. And Christians may operate from this same principle because it's supported by scripture.

15. How do property rights relate to human rights? I thought humans weren't property.

It may sound odd that we would speak about human rights in terms of property rights. Isn't the argument against slavery, for example, that human beings are *not* property? We completely agree that slavery—owning *another* human—is both a sin and a rights violation. However, the reason why this is the case is because each individual *already* owns themself, and therefore no one else has a legitimate claim to own them. We call this self-ownership. You are your own property.

We then come to own things outside of ourselves through the just acquisition of ownership of scarce resources. This is an extension of our self-ownership. Humans have been called by God to "be fruitful and multiply" (Gen. 1:28; 9:1; 9:7; 35:11; Jer. 23:3). Though the immediate sense of these verses are most obviously about human procreation, we also fulfill this call through our own creative work. Biblical theologian, Dr. Meredith G. Kline in *Kingdom Prologue* notes,

> "The procreation mandate was accompanied by the command to work. [Humankind] must labor to secure from [their] environment its life supporting stores for

[the] multiplying race... [Humans were] to subdue the earth and rule its creatures. Human labor was to be an exercise of [humanity's] dominion and a march of royal conquest.... Appropriation of earth's riches for the cultivation of [humankind] was to be achieved through [humans'] cultivation of the earth."

We acquire things found in nature and mix them with our labor to create new things.

This very concept, articulated by libertarian philosophers and Austrian economists, is illustrated for us in Deuteronomy 8:10-18. This passage references the wealth God gave his people as land, food, homes they build, and herds and flocks. It references part of that wealth is the multiplying of these things, the fact that human action has played a role in the production of these things, and that God is responsible for giving us the ability to produce it all. Add to this the prohibition in the 10 Commandments not to steal and murder, and we can see that we have a God-given right to our property, including that of ourselves.

These new things are our property by virtue of our own self-ownership. And as Matthew 20:15 and Acts 5:4 point out, it is lawful for us to do what we want with our own property, including selling and buying. So the foundations of human rights are very clearly indicated by what God gives us: our life, our ability to produce, the products of our labor, and the multiplicity of those things. We are stewards of these things in our relation to God, but owners of these things in relation to others.

So no one can claim to own you, nor lawfully sell you. Who owns you? Well, you do! And no one may make claims against the products of your labor; those are rightfully given to you by God because you produced them. The ultimate human right and the ultimate property right are one in the same: self-ownership.

16. But doesn't 1 Corinthians 6:19 explicitly state we do not own ourselves? Doesn't God own all things?

The world and everything in it are God's to do with as he pleases (Ps. 24:1, Deut. 10:14). There is no claim against God that would have any merit; he rightly owns it all (Job 41:11). Indeed, it was by an act of divine sovereignty that God entrusted this physical world to humanity's stewardship (Gen. 2:15).

In relation to God, we are stewards who are ultimately responsible to our master for what he has seen fit to entrust to us. However, in relation to each other, we are self-owners and owners of our own property.

This arrangement is not arbitrary, but rather it reveals the very wisdom of God. God has entrusted creation to humanity, and scripture affirms the institution of property ownership for managing that creation. Property rights reduce conflict over scarce resources. In this fallen world, we live in a state of scarcity and decay. It takes work to get the natural world to yield up the things we need to survive (Gen. 3:19). When property rights are reliably respected, that struggle for survival is made less burdensome. Property rights incentivize hard work and enable responsible planning for future needs (Prov. 6:6–11, 13:22). Biblical commandments against stealing and punishments for theft prohibiting theft logically affirm the legitimacy and necessity of personal property rights.

17. But if humans are stewards, how are we held accountable in our stewardship?

Human beings have often squandered the blessings that God has given us. Social institutions should reward productive activities and punish wasteful ones. The best institution for the maintenance of those favorable incentives is called the market. The market—when allowed to function freely—works to reallocate scarce resources to their best and highest uses for the satisfaction of human wants and needs, away from wasteful or inefficient uses.

In state institutions, resources are budgeted based on the subjective or ideological predilections of elected officials and bureaucrats. Government agencies distribute resources based on political rather than economic concerns. No matter how brilliant and well-intended the bureaucrats are, they simply cannot successfully aggregate and analyze all of the market information necessary to rationally plan the economy. Government planning is not necessarily malicious, but it is fundamentally clumsier than market-based planning.

Far from being a promoter of good stewardship, government social policy incentivizes poor decisionmaking and too often rewards and reinforces destructive behavior. This is not limited to one type of government; central planners of every political flavor fall short of the mark. On the global scale, governments are also the worst polluters in the world, and experiments in compulsory communism and collective ownership of natural resources have been environmental and humanitarian disasters. (For more, see Chapter 12)

18. The book of Acts says the early church shared things in common (Acts 2:42-47; 4:32). Doesn't this go against the idea of property rights?

Some progressive Christian groups argue that because the early church "held all things in common," property rights are not a Christian ideal and that, therefore, libertarianism is incompatible with Christianity. But this biblical example is insufficient proof of such a claim. Acts 2 might indicate that the early church was a small communal collective who made choices toward their collective good, but the conclusion that it is intended for the church more broadly ignores several key points:

1. The community was voluntary. We read in Acts 2:46 that they did this "with gladness."

2. The phrase "held all things in common" doesn't indicate whether they had some sort of intra-communal stewardship arrangements.

3. Ownership is implied in the phrase "sold their possessions and property." You can't sell what you don't own. While we don't get the full picture of all they did in this short passage, we do get the impression that they had property to begin with; otherwise they wouldn't be able to sell what they had.

It is also important to recognize that when the Bible discusses communal sharing, such as Acts 4:32, it is not indicative or suggestive of a legal arrangement, but a newly formed community centered around a common purpose. There is no reason to believe we are meant to apply this model to a nation-state, especially one comprised of those who are not committed to the same Gospel.

Additionally, it's notable that in Acts 5, Annanias and Sapphira's sin was not a lack of sharing, but in their lie. This is at least a small nod toward some semblance of stewardship required by those within the community itself.

For more on why this scenario isn't a model for a national or global economy, see Question 69.

19. Libertarianism just seems like a selfish philosophy to me.

Libertarianism is a philosophy that promotes *self-interest*, so it's easy to confuse this with selfishness. Selfishness implies a disregard for others. So the question then is, *does libertarianism promote a general disregard for others?* The short answer is, no.

Self-interested acts that disregard others by violating the NAP are considered criminal. There may be self-interested actions, which do not violate the NAP, that others would not choose for themselves and yet influence how they have to choose differently. This is simply the way life works. In our view, the individual and the community are of equal importance; we are individuals living in communities with one another, yet one is not more important than the other. Some people are inclined to believe that any self-interest is inherently selfish and therefore immoral. So let's consider what a completely altruistic world looks like.

Imagine a society where you could never say, 'no.' Where everyone belongs to everyone else and is meant to serve others. Any form of self-interest is considered selfish - a disregard for others in the community who have a right to your good will. Aldous Huxley's 1932 novel, *Brave New World*, depicts this utopian-dystopian world where all forms of self-interest are considered selfish. The implications of this sort of society turn out to be very anti-Christian with no monogamy, no family, no church, no love, and no privacy. Christianity is not opposed to self-interest. It is opposed to the general disregard of others. But the world Huxley predicted shows us what happens when we disregard self-interest and the individual right to choose. We are in fact acting selfishly, with disregard for others, when we don't acknowledge others' right to choose according to their self-interest. So we must consider self-interest as distinct from selfishness.

When two individuals voluntarily trade with one another, they do so from self-interest and the results are mutually beneficial. If it wasn't beneficial to both parties, they would voluntarily choose not to trade. As individuals within a community voluntarily trade, communities then voluntarily interact with one another. This too is for mutually beneficial ends *as a result* of individual self-interest. Libertarianism promotes regard for others through the principles of self-ownership, the NAP, and voluntary (mutually-beneficial) exchanges and associations.

20. Libertarianism feels too individualistic to be compatible with Christianity.

Libertarianism is neither individualist nor collectivist, though it's understandable that one might see it as individualistic, given that we begin with self-ownership and place such importance on individual human action. In fact, Murray Rothbard rightly pointed out that no libertarian thinker ever claimed an 'atomistic' view of the individual. But libertarianism doesn't stop there. When we pan out from the individual to see multiple individuals acting and interacting with each other, then we see communities form. Communities are voluntary associations of individuals. So individuals can interact with individuals, individuals can choose to work together in communities, communities of individuals can interact with other communities, and so on. Neither individuals nor communities are more basic than, or have their origin in, the other. The beautiful part of this process is that it is spontaneous—that is, there is no mastermind centrally planning this process.

So is this compatible with Christianity?

Well, it certainly seems that Christianity was formed this way. Christianity started with a single individual: Jesus Christ (John 1:1). His interactions with other individuals (especially the Twelve) formed communities who then formed more communities called churches. The individuals of these communities interacted with other communities, such as other churches, synagogues, and the pagan communities around them. These individuals were encouraged to live peaceably with others (Rom. 12:18) and to love their enemies (Matt. 5:43-48). And we carry on (or should carry on) this pattern today. There are no human masterminds centrally planning these communities. There's certainly room for theological explanations of God's providential work behind it all.

Libertarianism doesn't artificially bind Christians morally where Christ has left them free (Gal. 5). So not only do we think libertarianism is compatible with Christianity, but it actually affirms and works with what appears to be God's design for societal order.

Further Reading

Healing Our World: In an Age of Aggression | Mary Ruwart (Sunstar Press, 2003)

Called to Freedom: Why You Can be Christian and Libertarian | Elise Daniel, Ed. (Wipf & Stock, 2017)

For a New Liberty: The Libertarian Manifesto | Murray Rothbard (Mises Institute, 1973)

The Ethics of Liberty | Murray Rothbard (Mises Institute, 1982)

Libertarianism: What Everyone Needs to Know | Jason Brennan (Oxford University Press, 2012)

Turn Neither to the Right nor to the Left | D. Eric Schansberg (Alertness Ltd., 2003)

Liberty Defined | Ron Paul (Grand Central Publishing, 2012)

The Revolution: A Manifesto | Ron Paul (Grand Central Publishing, 2008)

The Market for Liberty Morris and Linda Tannehill (Mises Institute, 1970)

"How We Come to Own Ourselves" | Stephen Kinsella (Mises Institute, 2006)

3
WHAT IS GOVERNMENT?

"There is no such thing as Government with a capital G. There is only an arrangement which sets aside a small group of people and gives them the power to coerce all the rest of the people."

— Edmund Opitz

21. Isn't the government an institution created by God? How can a Christian square this truth with being anti-government?

Satan was originally created by God too, but we do not presume to think that makes Satan good or that everything Satan does is approved or justified by God. Consider that even in the case of Job, God was permitting Satan's actions but not approving. Likewise, we can recognize that God created everything in this world, including the state, but this fact neither makes the state a good institution nor justifies its activities.

God gives no special privileges of position to do evil or to let ends justify means (James 2, Rom. 2:11, Rom. 3:8). Therefore, we should oppose institutions that claim such power to coerce and the privilege to commit aggression against others—which is inherently what states do. This does not mean we take up arms and fight every chance we have against such institutions, but rather, we act peacefully to persuade and help people realize that there are better ways to organize ourselves and solve problems than committing acts of aggression against each other.

God has given his creation a measure of self-determination: the ability to "choose this day whom you will serve" (Josh. 24:15). We see Satan as choosing to rebel against God and thus fall from grace, and God allowed it. Humans commit a similar rebellion through the institutionalization of aggressive force—that is, the formation of the state—and God allows it as well. Romans 13 gives us an idea of how to act within it, but the passage does not morally justify its existence or behaviors.

22. Okay, so maybe not all governments are established by God. But isn't the state needed to keep sinful people under control?

All people are sinful, but does this mean we need the state to control all people?

There are certainly those who would agree that people need to be controlled. One of the key philosophers who advocated this idea was Thomas Hobbes. Hobbes maintained that individuals pose a direct threat to each other, thereby making the existence of the state a necessity for maintaining order. He believed that power to govern equally distributed among individuals was a motivator for people to attack one another, and that power held centrally, by either an organization or a single person, resulted in peaceful cooperation. James Madison echoed this in his famous quip, "If men were angels, no government would be necessary."

But since libertarian Christians recognize that all people are sinful and have a propensity toward corrupting power, we disagree that the state is a necessary apparatus for tempering sinful behavior. Indeed, the last thing we want to do is concentrate monopoly power in the hands of sinners. Instead, it's the role of the church to encourage moral behavior, and the role of the Holy Spirit to sanctify us, in part, toward that end. Contrary to popular belief, "legislating morality" is outside the scope of God-ordained civil governance.

To create the conditions for human flourishing society needs civil governance. Civil governance is the administration of civil justice, which is based on the legitimate use of coercion. The initiation or first use of coercion is always illegitimate, regardless of whether it's an individual acting alone or people acting in the name of governing authority. So straight away we see that it's improper for civil governance to control anything through the initiation of force. Instead, civil governance can only be responsive, and only to previously (and thus improperly) initiated coercion.

23. Sure, the state isn't great at managing society, but surely they "keep the peace," right?

It's helpful to understand what is meant by "keep the peace." This phrase has become a rather meaningless idiom. We used to call our judges "justices of the peace" and our law enforcement officers "peace officers." Supporters of law enforcement often (and, in our view, mistakenly) associate Matthew 5:9 ("blessed are the peacemakers") with law enforcement officers. But it's a contradiction to attribute "peacekeeper" to people who regularly initiate force and violence upon others.

If the state exists to "keep the peace," then they sure aren't doing a very good job of it. Criminal justice reform is a regular campaign issue. On the one hand, there are problems with the administrative side: police brutality, no-knock raids, corrupt or careless judges, etc. On the other hand, there are problems with the effectiveness of the policies: high recidivism rates, mandatory minimums, overcrowding and rising cost of prisons, etc.

How much peace we enjoy today is really due to market forces and not because of (or in spite of) government policies?

There are a couple of ways we can conceive of civil governance as "keeping the peace." One classic metaphor is the "night watchman." Another is a "referee." Either way, the peacekeeping role of civil governance necessitates the impartiality of the peacekeeper in a given dispute. Historically, the difficulty has always been holding the peacekeeper accountable when disputes arise involving them. This is part of the ongoing dialogue between libertarian anarchists and libertarian minarchists (see Question 25). The aim of both, however, is that civil governance is only successful in "keeping the peace" when it's properly and effectively limited.

24. If the government doesn't make laws, how will people know what authority to obey?

The fundamental principles of self-ownership and non-aggression are self-evidently true (see Questions 14-16). In other words, people intuitively know them. In fact, you'll find that arguments against them are derived from premises which assume they're true. How can this be? God's creational order entails laws written into the fabric of reality. This involves physical laws (e.g., the law of gravity), but also involves normative laws (e.g., "you shall not murder," Ex. 20:13). God's law is written on the hearts of humankind (Rom. 2:15), even if they try to suppress the truth of it (Rom. 1:18).

Beyond this, disputes arise as human beings come in contact and interact with one another. Along with voluntary human action comes disagreement; this is inevitable. There are two ways people would know what authority to obey if the government didn't create new law: contracts and dispute resolutions.

First, with contracts, the rules governing parties are established at the onset of the relationship. This is useful when dealing with an exchange of services (if you do this, then I'll give you that), where stipulations aren't self-evident and therefore need to be defined. But contracts cannot foresee all possible outcomes and disputes arise. For these disputes, resolutions need to be made by third-party arbitration. These might be courts or private agencies. Part of any good contract you find today is an agreement to use third-party arbitration in the event a dispute arises. So our society is already acclimated to this form of governance.

If the dispute happens to be a common problem, then the resolution could become common practice where it's effective and upholds the property rights of the parties involved. In our current system, we might refer to this as "case law." And even case law can (and would) be challenged in a libertarian society. No doubt, there will need to be a way of keeping track of effective dispute resolutions, which means there will be a market need for impartial record keeping. Some have suggested that blockchain technology could serve this purpose. But whatever the solution, the need for contracts and resolution necessitates a market response, not a monopoly response from a state government.

25. Do libertarians believe any and every government is illegitimate?

This is a tricky question. Libertarians are a diverse bunch situated across an ideological spectrum. And we have to talk about what a "government" is.

Some libertarians advocate for a government in the form of a minimal, "night watchman" state. These libertarians believe that a few things are best provided through a limited state; usual examples include so-called "public goods" like roads, national defense, and a court system. Other than those limited public functions, minarchist libertarians believe that markets can reliably serve the needs of society.

Other libertarians reject the need for the state altogether. These libertarians believe that public goods can be provided by competing enterprises operating on a voluntary, profit-motivated basis. They are pessimistic about the prospects for keeping limited states within their appointed bounds. These libertarian anarchists want markets to be entirely self-regulated.

But one thing that all libertarians do believe in is some form of governance. Libertarians all believe in keeping the peace and protecting the vulnerable. We just have different ideas about how those important functions might be carried out.

26. Wait a sec, are you saying there's a difference between governance and government?

In English, the word "government" has changed over time. The famous author and professing Christian J.R.R. Tolkien complained in a letter to his son that "Government is an abstract noun meaning the art and process of governing and it should be an offence to write it with a capital G or so as to refer to people."

Contrary to Tolkien's preferences, the word "government" in common usage more often refers to government entities, not to the process of government. It makes sense to use the term "governance" to refer to what Tolkien believed "government" should have meant all along. The distinction is important, because one refers to a noble social goal, and the other refers to a group of people who may or may not be so noble.

Governance, in essence, is about restraining injustice. Christians should care very much about justice, because we know God loves justice (see Question 12). Violent crimes like armed robbery and kidnapping are not the only sorts of injustices that we should avoid; more mundane evils are still matters of great concern to God. The Bible tells us that honest dealing is pleasing to God (Prov. 16:11). He condemns those who use dishonest weights and measures (Prov. 20:23, Mic. 6:11). Employers who withhold just wages from workers and build up earthly palaces with dishonest gain will be judged by God (Jer. 22:13–15, James 5:4). The ancient Israelites in the time of Amos were judged nationally, in part, for tolerating perjury against the innocent and abuse of the poor (Amos 2:6).

Punishing evildoers to avenge wrongdoing is something that Christians are ultimately called to trust God for (Rom. 12:19). God does use earthly authorities as a means for punishing evildoers (Rom. 13:4). He repeatedly used the pagan governments of the other nations to chasten backsliding Israel (Judg. 2:20–23). However, nowhere is God's instruction to justice-hungry believers that we should use secular government to carry out our work as the body of Christ. Remember that when Gideon was given the opportunity to rule, he refused and reminded the Israelites that God was their ruler (Judg. 8:22–23) Not only did Christ refuse Satan's offer of the Kingdoms of the world, but Christ also resisted the Jewish Zealots who believed the coming messiah would be a political king who would overthrow Israel's oppressors.

27. Why do governments need to be limited? Shouldn't they be able to do whatever it takes to keep the peace?

If government is meant to keep the peace, that presupposes that we value peace. As Christians, we should! If we are in Christ, he gives us an internal peace even as we face the trials of this world (John 14:27). Christians should desire agreeable, peaceful relations with everyone, in part because that is how the lost can see God's love through us (Heb. 12:14, 2 Cor. 13:11). We are called to be peacemakers (Matt. 5:9). If a member of the body is easily angered or provoked to violence, scripture warns us these character traits disqualify that person from service in church leadership (Titus 1:7–8).

A familiar quotation often attributed to George Washington warns that, "Government is not reason, it is not eloquence—it is force. Like fire it is a dangerous servant and a fearful master."

Violence is the opposite of peace. It destroys resources, relationships, and human lives. As Christian believers and followers of the Prince of Peace, we should be gravely skeptical of violence and reluctant to resort to it. If the defining characteristic of government is force, it stands to reason that government is not a tool Christians should be fond of using.

28. The government is a special entity. It sounds like you're holding it to the same ethics as individuals have to obey.

Every proper authority in society is necessarily limited. The authority of parents is limited to their own family. The authority of church officers is limited to the church. The authority of an employer is limited to the sphere of business. Government is not an exception. To treat it as an unlimited touchstone of societal order is to make an idol of it. Libertarians believe that we should evaluate questions of justice uniformly, regardless of whether a person is an agent of the state or a private individual. The American Declaration of Independence recited a radical claim about governments "deriving their just powers from the consent of the governed."

Consent is the crucial difference between competitive boxing and criminal battery. Consent is the essential ingredient that must be present in order for any government power to be just. The claim that consent is relevant even for the sovereign logically implies that justice is not just a matter of what government says. Justice is a standard not subject to modification by any mortal person.

For Christians, these claims should ring true. The Bible tells us that God's law does not ever change (Luke 16:17). God's law of love applies equally to every person made in his image, prince and pauper alike. "God is no respecter of persons" (Acts 10:34b, KJV), which means he doesn't play favorites. Christ-followers must be opposed to the perversion of justice to recognize social station, wealth, or for any other reason (James 2:1–4, 8–9).

29. What sort of legal order would a libertarian support?

Libertarians prefer markets to bureaucracy. The world we live in today is largely dominated by state bureaucracies. We usually think of "law and order" as being a product of government. In spite of government courts dominating the legal market, there is a flourishing market for alternative dispute resolution services. Negotiation, mediation, and arbitration are important means for avoiding or resolving disputes that would otherwise go in front of a judge.

The efficiency of private mediation and arbitration has led to legislation in some jurisdictions that encourage or even require disputing parties to participate in mediation before asking the court to solve their problems. These services offer predictable outcomes to parties, they control costs, and they can be more private than litigation in government courts. A report published by the Economic Policy Institute in September 2017 claimed that the share of the American workforce subject to mandatory arbitration agreements had risen from about 2 percent in 1992 to over 55 percent by 2017. Purchasers of airline tickets, luxury cruise berths, and other relatively expensive consumer services will find that they, too, are subject to mandatory arbitration clauses should a dispute arise with their service provider.

A libertarian legal order would utilize these effective, private dispute resolution methods instead of relying on a centralized, monopolistic government court system. Competition between arbitration firms already exists today. In a free market in legal services, this competition would continue to promote efficiency and reach reasonable, predictable outcomes. If a party failed to honor his legal obligations, adjudication of that failure would likely impact his creditworthiness and future business prospects.

Further Reading

Civil Government: Its Origin, Mission, and Destiny, and the Christian's Relation to It | David Lipscomb (Gospel Advocate Publishing Company, 1889)

"Theology Doesn't Begin and End With Romans 13" | Norman Horn (Libertarian Christian Institute, 2013)

The Enterprise of Law: Justice Without the State | Bruce Benson (Independent Institute, 2013)

Chaos Theory | Robert P. Murphy (Ludwig von Mises Institute, 2002)

Creation in the Image of the Glory Spirit | Meredith G. Kline (1980)

"Privatizing the Adjudication of Disputes" | Edward P. Stringham & Bryan Caplan (Theoretical Inquiries in Law, Vol. 9, No. 2, 2008)

The Quest for Community | Robert Nisbet (Intercollegiate Studies Institute, 2010)

"The Church of Christ and World-Powers" | David Lipscomb (ed. Norman Horn)

"The Growing Use of Mandatory Arbitration" | Alexander J.S. Colvin (Economic Policy Institute, 2017)

4

DOES A FREE SOCIETY HAVE LIMITS?

"Rightful liberty is unobstructed action according to our will within limits drawn around us by the equal rights of others. I do not add 'within the limits of the law' because law is often but the tyrant's will, and always so when it violates the rights of the individual."

— Thomas Jefferson

30. Shouldn't there be limits on individual freedom? People can't just do whatever they want without consequences!

As Christians, we know that sin has consequences both in this temporal life and in eternity. A person who diligently works to provide for future needs will usually receive favorable consequences from his actions: he and his family will eat! Labor is often unpleasant, but it brings the joyful reward of the harvest. "Those who sow in tears shall reap with shouts of joy! He who goes out weeping, bearing the seed for sowing, shall come home with shouts of joy, bringing his sheaves with him." (Ps. 126:5–6, ESV)

A person who is lazy and irresponsible will eventually be both humbled and hungry (Prov. 10:4, 13:4; 20:4). The sin of idleness is not just something that has consequences for the idle person. Scripture warns that failure to provide for one's family members, especially one's own household, is a denial of the Christian faith (1 Tim. 5:8).

There are many other vices that are currently treated as crimes by the state: activities related to drug and alcohol abuse, prostitution, gambling, and so forth. As Christians, we should counsel our brothers and sisters to avoid polluting their bodily temples. We should encourage wise stewardship instead of frivolous frittering away of the resources with which God entrusts us. But the Bible does not teach us to use violence to exhort others to good works. Indeed, strict, external enforcement of rules about touching, tasting, and eating forbidden things does not help to restrain sensual indulgence (Col. 2:16–23). Using violence for reasons other than responding to violent aggressors is not a proportionate response to wrongdoing (Lev. 24:19–21).

31. What limitations do I have as an individual under libertarianism?

Libertarianism only speaks to what is just or unjust for an individual to do. The boundary between justice and injustice is based on the ownership of property, including your own body. Libertarianism categorically rejects violations of other people's property rights as wrong. However, if an act does not violate another person's rights, it is not "unlibertarian," which is to say that it is not an injustice. Libertarians agree that the use of force against others is only permissible if they are aggressors whose actions violate the rights of others. Otherwise, libertarianism leaves the individual free to choose what to do with his time and property.

But remember, libertarianism only speaks to what should be legal. As Christian libertarians, we recognize that a thing's being lawful is not enough to make it good. Believers must also consider whether a particular choice is spiritually expedient; that is, whether it glorifies God (1 Cor. 6:12, 1 Cor. 10:23–29). Justice tells us what people can be compelled to do or not do.

The teachings of our Lord in scripture and through the moving of the Holy Spirit show us how we ought to live in order to please and glorify him (2 Tim. 3:16, 1 Cor. 2:6–16).

32. What keeps others from victimizing me under libertarianism?

Governance is a lot bigger than government. There is a thriving market for a variety of accountability and protection products and services. The invention of financial bookkeeping made sophisticated financial audits possible. Computer software has made managing these records and auditing them faster and easier. Many journalists have made careers out of revealing scandals of public concern or reviewing products to expose the dangerous and unreliable ones.

Underwriters Laboratories has been a leading product safety testing and certification firm for more than a century, and it earns billions of dollars every year doing it, largely motivated by concerns of insurance companies that would lose money if policyholders suffer a loss. Burglar alarms, security cameras, fences, locks, and self-defense products are all produced by entrepreneurs serving the demand for protection against wrongdoers.

Make no mistake: we live in a fallen world. In this fallen world, we will face a variety of perils to which we apply our God-given talents and material resources. Libertarians do not promise a utopia. Libertarian Christians benefit from the insight of scripture. We know that a perfect human society is not possible so long as the world is in the thrall of sin. As Christians, we should prepare for tomorrow with prudence and diligence. We must be careful, though, to always put our trust in God, not in our own strength or in the plans of secular leaders. We do not always know how God is planning to work things out. However, we know our God is good and that he will lead us if we acknowledge him and look to him for guidance (Prov. 3:5–6).

33. What if other people don't like what I do or how I live?

People often disagree with each other about what life ought to look like. As Christians, we believe that we ought to live as Christ taught us to live. Scripture tells us that the world hated Christ and that it hates Christ followers, too (John 15:18-19). Despite living in a world that hates us, we should do our best to live at peace with everyone (Rom. 12:18). In his letter to the Philippian faithful, Paul reminded them of Jesus's self-humbling, self-sacrificial example. Loving peace and avoiding disputes are habits that are practically beneficial "in the midst of a crooked and perverse nation." They allow us to be bright lights in a dark and sinful world (Phil. 2:5–16).

We are to be so conflict-averse—and loving towards others—that Christ admonished us to respond to presumptuous demands with a charitable response that goes above and beyond what is demanded (Matt. 5:38–42, Luke 6:27–36). This is commanded even towards our enemies (Matt. 5:43–48; Luke 6:32–36).

Paul exhorted the faithful in Corinth to abstain from using secular courts to sue other believers (1 Cor. 1:1–11). Jesus told us the appropriate steps for making a godly appeal to an offending brother or sister in Christ, and that process is in the context of a local fellowship of believers (Matt. 18:16–17).

34. What about people who have more wealth? They can buy votes and rig the system in their favor!

It is true that wealthy political donors can obtain ready access to elected policymakers in a way that other people cannot. This is true despite complicated campaign finance laws and limitations on how and when money may be donated. Taxing wealthy people more cannot change that—they will still have plenty of things that others want.

Even where campaign contributions are not at issue, lobbyists often get their way for another, seemingly benign reason: lobbyists are usually experts in their policy areas. Politicians learn to rely on lobbyists to efficiently explain complex legal and policy issues to them. It should be unsurprising when the "students" later reach the same policy positions as their "teachers."

Lord Acton, a 19th century English historian, famously said that "power tends to corrupt." The libertarian solution is to rely more on markets and to rely less on political policymaking. Markets are ultimately controlled by consumer preference and the realities of business. Though individuals make mistakes sometimes, when they are engaged in market activities the personal consequences of failure naturally motivate them to exercise great care.

Economists sometimes refer to a problem called "moral hazard." Moral hazard exists when a decisionmaker has an incentive to increase risk because they are not directly impacted by the consequences of that risk. For example, many libertarians are concerned that banks engage in riskier conduct because of the prospect of government bailouts. The decisions politicians make are chiefly about other people's resources, not their own. Private entrepreneurs and investors are financially accountable for their actions in a way that politicians never are.

Christians know that perverting justice, especially for money, is an abomination to God (Deut. 16:18–20). Politicizing and bureaucratizing justice does not promote equality before the law. In fact, political and bureaucratic incentives can facilitate further injustice. We know this from economic theory. We also know it from scripture (Ecc. 5:8–9).

Further Reading

Religion: Foundation of the Free Society | Edmund Opitz (Foundation for Economic Education, 1996)

The Free Society | Laurence Vance (Vance Publications, 2018)

The Voluntary City: Choice, Community, and Civil Society | David Beito, Peter Gordon, and Alex Tabarrok (University of Michigan Press, 2002)

The Art of Community | Spencer Heath MacCallum (Institute for Humane Studies, 1970)

Markets Without Limits | Jason Brennan and Peter M. Jaworski (Routledge, 2016)

Myth of the Rational Voter: Why Democracies Choose Bad Policies | Bryan Caplan (Princeton University Press, 2011)

Bureaucracy | Ludwig von Mises (Mises Institute, 1944)

Anarchy, State, and Utopia | Robert Nozick (Basic Books, 2013)

5

IS CAPITALISM PROBLEMATIC?

"I believe a man is happier, and happy in a richer way, if he has 'the freeborn mind.' But I doubt whether he can have this without economic independence, which the new society is abolishing. For economic independence allows an education not controlled by Government; and in adult life it is the man who needs, and asks, nothing of Government who can criticize its acts and snap his fingers at its ideology."

— C.S. Lewis

35. How can a Christian support the pursuit of profit when the Bible says "the love of money is a root of all kinds of evil" (1 Tim. 6:10)?

Libertarian Christians firmly acknowledge that the pursuit of money as an end in itself is sinful and damaging to oneself and to others. In the Bible, money is not to be an end in itself, because anything good and useful that is made ultimate is actually the source problem. It is not wrong to seek more money because you have very little and need to make ends meet, or because you wish to provide meaningful work for others. Money used as a tool is wise stewardship. Money as an end-in-itself is where we go astray.

Seeking profit is not, economically speaking, a matter of the why, as in the Bible. In an economic sense, pursuing profit is another way of saying we are utilizing scarce resources to create value for ourselves and others. This does not guarantee good results, but the profit-and-loss system signals to humans that resources are being used properly, not abused.

Pursuing profit is what everyone does every day when we choose to go to work. From manual laborers to high-level managerial work, everybody seeks an income which covers their expenses, plus some. What is done with that "plus some" is up to each person to decide. Charity, reinvestment, savings, spending—all these are options each individual must decide is right for them.

36. Doesn't capitalism create winners and losers through competition and conflict?

The most popular misunderstanding about free markets results from a misunderstanding of the term *competition*, probably because we use it in sports where there are winners and losers in a zero-sum game. Yet not all sports are zero-sum (some competitions have various tiers of "winners"), and the free market is especially not a zero-sum game.

A better way to think about competition is that it drives people to pursue the best interests of their customers in ways that rival other businesses. That is, good businesses compete in how much better they can serve customers, and customers reward the businesses that serve them better. This is not a situation of conflict, nor is it an either/or outcome. Even the "lesser" of the two businesses can still win a different customer base. And in reality, most of us want bad businesses to fail so owners can appropriate their resources to more productive uses for society.

In reality, free competition in the market aids in creating a more vibrant and dynamic economy where the needs of everyone are met to a greater degree. When the state is involved, it inherently sows discord and breeds conflict because it causes businesses to compete for attention, favors, and special privileges. This kind of competition is a destructive force in an economy.

37. Doesn't capitalism promote consumerism and materialism?

Christians rightly oppose that which engenders greed and creates an insatiable appetite for more. Critics of capitalism believe that because businesses are always pursuing profit by trying to please consumers, both producers and consumers are always wanting more and more in an endless cycle of materialistic hedonism. They say this creates an unhealthy economy.

Yet at its heart, capitalism is about creating new and innovative ways of using scarce resources for human flourishing. The very term "capital" denotes the use, not depletion, of resources. It is unfortunate that our modern Western economy is labeled "capitalism" because there are large parts of it that depend on the demand for more. In fact, the dominant economic theory most at play is Keynesianism, which is a consumerist version of the economy. It is inaccurately named "capitalism."

What critics of capitalism often ignore is the significantly better outcomes for human flourishing that have resulted over the past 200 years. Yes, some people are materialistic, but that isn't a guaranteed outcome. Capitalism has created a space for humans to flourish materially, and many are now ready to think about and ponder deeper spiritual realities.

38. What about the inequalities that capitalism creates?

Economic inequality has always existed wherever there have been economies. In pre-capitalist days, having wealth often (but not always) entailed exploiting others who then remained poor. This is one reason we see so many admonitions against wealth in the Bible. It is also why many early church leaders and theologians decry wealth. It is only recently that being wealthy has *not* been associated with unjust acquisition of wealth but instead with the indication that mutually beneficial trade is occurring.

Under free market capitalism, wealth must be obtained by effectively and efficiently providing value to others in exchange for their money. Whenever inequality indicates that the few are exploiting others and leaving them worse off, we should stand against it. But under conditions where everyone is better off and some are "more better off," we can appreciate, if not applaud, the gains through exchange.

Christians are often concerned about the wellbeing of others, yet it is all too common that concern over inequality is not about the wellbeing of those with less but a suppressed envy that arises because of the perceived reasons behind the injustice.

We must be mindful that we are not suppressing our envy when we advocate for the wellbeing of others. All too often the concern over inequality is not about the wellbeing of those with less but the perceived reason behind the perceived injustice. For example, while the purchasing power of the average worker's wages has improved dramatically for several decades, the top 1% have seen even greater gains. Many have pointed out that this is the reason to institute redistributive schemes to rectify the perceived injustice of inequality, even though everyone has gained financially (see Question 40).

39. Is economic growth all libertarians care about?

Economic growth is not merely about the money in our bank accounts or the GDP of an economy. While those *can* be indications of prosperity or growth, they are just that: indicators. Real economic growth only occurs when scarce resources are put to use in increasing ways. This happens through free exchange, a profit-and-loss system, and innovation in labor and capital, and results in an increased material well-being.

Because libertarian Christians care about freedom from violence, we have respect for private property (see Question 14) and adherence to the non-aggression principle (see Question 13). This leads us to believe that freedom of exchange should be permitted in an open market. Libertarian Christians would strongly support the idea that when individuals are free to do commerce with one another under the conditions of peace and voluntarism, we should expect the economy to grow and the well-being of individuals to improve.

40. Why are poor people still poor when our country has so much wealth?

Why people are poor has many complicated answers which constitute a mixture of personal and social explanations. We should always reserve judgment on individuals for their circumstances in life, regardless of how much we think we know about their world. When we consider why any particular individual, family, or even community is poor, we must remember it is possible to factor in both individual responsibility *and* institutional injustices that contribute to the underlying reasons.

An additional layer to this question is asking, "What do you mean by 'poor'?" Absolute poverty has been falling for decades, both nationally and globally. Those who are poor by today's standards have access to or possess the types of goods and services only available to the wealthy half a century ago. This is not to make light of the plight of those on the margins, but to suggest that what constitutes poverty is a moving target.

To ask "why are people still poor" by adding "when our country has so much wealth" is to make an assumed connection between the wealth of some and the lack of others. There may be a connection, but assessing this requires an empirical analysis of the economies involved. But even if there is a small causal connection, this does not explain the reasons for lack in our world. It also commits what many economists call the "fixed pie fallacy."

The fixed pie fallacy is the assumption that the economy is a certain size and that the portions are distributed in such a way that a larger slice for you means a smaller slice for me. If the economy were like this, we could have cause for concern over inequality. But consider this: was the "pie" in 1870 as big as in 2020? Nobody would claim it's the same size pie. It's clearly a larger pie.

41. Aren't markets inherently unstable and detrimental to human flourishing?

We need to point out what the mainstream media means by markets and what we mean by markets. If you've listened to the financial talking heads on cable television news shows, you might believe markets are a reference to Wall Street, or the Stock Market. But "the market" for libertarians, are *all* instances of human beings making voluntary exchanges for mutually beneficial ends. This includes the Stock Market, but also includes you and me and the exchanges we make every day.

So the market is actually quite stable. Though there will always be a natural ebb and flow in the market, the real culprit of market instability is government intervention either through economic regulation or monetary policy. For example, since the establishment of the Federal Reserve Bank, the boom and bust cycle of the economy has become a normal feature. Ironically, when the economy is in the bust phase of the cycle, capitalism and "free markets" are blamed, but during the boom phase of the cycle, extolling the virtues of a market economy are rare. In fact, most people incorrectly believe America's current economic structure is the best example of "free market capitalism" the world has ever seen. It's really not. Investopedia correctly identifies America's economic system as a mixed economy; mixed between capitalism and socialism. Immediately blaming "the market" (or capitalism) for the problems in our economy is at best ignoring the socialist elements and at worst, a false cause fallacy. What libertarians and Austrian economists find upon closer analysis of these problems is that it's the socialist elements of the economy that are to blame for "market instability."

Intervention in the market itself is a hindrance to human flourishing. Human flourishing requires that we allow individuals to participate freely in an economy. When markets are free from interference, humans flourish.

Further Reading

Defending the Free Market: The Moral Case for a Free Economy | Robert Sirico (Regenery, 2012)

Economics in One Lesson | Henry Hazlitt (Currency, 1988)

Foundations of Economics: A Christian View | Shawn Ritenour (Wipf and Stock, 2010)

Counting the Cost: Christian Perspectives on Capitalism | Art Lindsley & Anne Bradley eds. (Abilene Christian University Press, 2017)

The Church and the Market | Thomas E. Woods, Jr. (Lexington Books, 2005)

Choice: Cooperation, Enterprise, and Human Action | Robert Murphy (Independent Institute, 2015)

How Capitalism Saved America | Thomas J. DiLorenzo (Crown Forum, 2005)

How Then Should We Work?: Rediscovering the Biblical Doctrine of Work | Hugh Whelchel (Institute for Faith, Work & Economics, 2012)

The Good of Affluence: Seeking God in a Culture of Wealth | John R. Schneider (Eerdmans, 2002)

Why It's OK to Want to Be Rich | Jason Brennan (Routledge, 2020)

The Spirit of Democratic Capitalism | Michael Novak (Madison Books, 1991)

6

WHAT ABOUT CHRISTIAN MORALS AND ETHICS?

My contention is that good men (not bad men) consistently acting upon that position would act as cruelly and unjustly as the greatest tyrants. They might in some respects act even worse. Of all tyrannies, a tyranny sincerely exercised for the good of its victims may be the most oppressive. It would be better to live under robber barons than under omnipotent moral busybodies. The robber baron's cruelty may sometimes sleep, his cupidity may at some point be satiated; but those who torment us for our own good will torment us without end for they do so with the approval of their own conscience.

— C.S. Lewis

42. Wouldn't I have to endorse prostitution if I'm a libertarian?

No.

Just because a behavior is legal doesn't make it moral or something anyone should condone. For those who might balk at the idea of legal prostitution, consider how we draw the distinction on abortion. It's easy for us to see how something can be legal and not moral. (Obviously this becomes disanalogous when we understand why abortion should not be legal either; see Chpater 11.)

Libertarianism draws a much sharper line between legality and morality—and not because we seek a more licentious society, as some have claimed. Many Christians believe the role of government is to legislate morality—that is, to prescribe moral rules for society over and above rights violations. Romans 13:4 is often used to hit home the idea that the role of government is to promote what is morally good and punish that which is morally wrong. Christian libertarians would certainly agree that all rights violations are morally wrong, but that's where we stop. Why?

Those behaviors that are morally wrong but are not rights violations in themselves, like prostitution, drug addiction, or suicide, are indicative of social ills or health problems that can be addressed by the free market (and the gospel). Prostitution, which is often connected to human trafficking (which is a rights violation!), usually occurs when women are in desperate situations. And often when they seek to escape prostitution, they wind up punished and exploited by the criminal justice system.

Alternatively, women who choose prostitution voluntarily cannot seek justice for rape, often because the authorities believe they deserved to be raped. Is that justice? We don't think so. So while Christian libertarians wouldn't endorse prostitution, we do believe that legalizing it will help women who want out to escape it, and women who want to stay in to at least get justice when rights violations occur.

43. If addictive/harmful drugs are legalized, doesn't that mean more people will use them?

It's true that people will use drugs if they're legal, but it's also true that drugs are used while they're illegal. Libertarianism doesn't deny that human beings are plagued with vices. But it does deny that vices rise to the level of criminal activity.

This, of course, doesn't answer the question of how society should handle vices like drug addiction. But just because libertarians don't want the government to handle drug addiction doesn't mean we don't want anything done about it at all. Quite the contrary.

There is a necessary distinction between government and other societal spheres. Often the objection to decriminalization stems from a moral question, not a legal one. If the goal is to reduce the use of drugs and our legal system doesn't consider drug use a crime, then drug addicts are free to seek market services to help them overcome their addiction.

Criminalizing drug use activity makes it more difficult for drug addicted users to get help. Criminalization doesn't prevent use. Studying it (rather than merely accosting the immorality of it), we find that decriminalization doesn't encourage more use; it encourages addiction recovery. Isn't that what we want in our society?

As Christians, we're called to respond to the world with grace and compassion (Zech. 7:9-10, 2 Cor. 1:3-4, Gal. 6:2, Eph. 4:32, Col. 3:12). Since criminalization of drug use only compounds the problem and doesn't achieve the ultimate goal, it stands to reason that the Christian response is through means that are proven to achieve the original intent of criminalization—the reduction of drug use in society—and that means decriminalization and promotion of market services for recovery.

44. What does a libertarian Christian suggest to keep greed in check in a truly free market?

Libertarianism is perceived to advocate for allowing people to do anything they want, regardless of the consequences. In most people's minds, this means letting people with a lot of money and power do things that disadvantage or oppress those who are not in those same positions.

What advocates of regulated markets claim is that government intervention is needed to keep greedy capitalists in check. That is, without some government regulations, the top 1 percent of earners would run roughshod over the 99 percent. What we find, however, is that the government regulatory agencies actually favor and protect the elite few in their regulatory measures. In other words, the regulations intended to keep greed in check actually enable it for those who cozy up to lawmakers and bureaucrats.

We're often left with the impression that a lack of government regulations means a lack of any regulation in the market. But this isn't so. The consumer acts to regulate the market. When a consumer purchases a good or service, they send signals to producers that the good or service is a market need. When consumers see unethical business practice and stop purchasing from a particular producer, they are sending a signal that they won't tolerate said practice.

If anything, libertarians are keenly aware of the dangers of economic elitists, but we also understand how these elites exploit regulatory agencies for their own gain. What we see is that the most efficient regulator of the market is the consumer, and an unregulated market really does level the playing field.

45. How do libertarian Christians account for "gay rights" or "women's rights"?

Libertarians don't demarcate rights based on group identity; there are only human rights. And as human beings, we all have the same rights. One reason group identity politics have become a problem is because of systemic rights violations related to particular groups of people. Women have had their rights systematically violated throughout history. That said, not all "rights" advocated for by these groups are indeed rights. When we treat rights this way, groups are set against each other. This is essentially how we get class warfare, except now it might be more accurate to call it social or identitarian warfare.

By reaffirming that all human beings have equal rights by virtue of their humanity, we resolve the conflict between these groups. Those groups who have been oppressed should have their human rights recognized. Those groups who claim that which are not rights can be peacefully corrected. The libertarian concept of human rights is the equalling of the playing field for all.

46. Fair enough, but what about marriage licenses? Marriage is defined by God but the state now recognizes marriage as a right for homosexuals and libertarians seem to agree.

The marriage license is a relatively new phenomenon in American history. It was first introduced because the government didn't approve of interracial marriage, and so required interracial couples to ask the government permission before getting married. The government would either approve their relationship or deny it. If approved, they received a license.

The marriage license doesn't signify a Christian marriage. A Christian marriage is a lifelong covenant between a man, a woman, and God. A marriage license is a temporal contract between you, your spouse, and the state — and God can be a witness if you choose (I'm sure he appreciates the consolation).

Even if you believe that gay marriage is biblical, the marriage license is not a biblical requirement for Christians to uphold the sanctity of this covenant. It is little more than a golden calf of the evangelical right. There is no need to idolize it.

The government has no legitimate authority to grant permission to voluntary adult relationships, despite their having asserted themselves to the contrary. The practical matters of marriage can be handled through contract law, essentially a kind of prenuptial agreement. Third party dispute agencies or the local magistrates can adjudicate these contracts should the need arise. But state-issued licensing is not a bastion of freedom; it's a tool of oppression. In fact, clergy who cooperate with marriage licensing turn out to be unpaid agents of the state, enforcing a rule that is extra-biblical.

Even if some libertarians condone homosexual marriage, true equality means not having to ask the government permission to exercise your rights. Regardless of where you stand on gay marriage, the most optimal option is to abolish the marriage license altogether. We don't need the government's permission to enter into a covenant with God, and God will sort in his eyes who is married and who is not.

47. If society becomes more libertarian, won't this mean a cultural collapse into hedonism?

There will always be those who attempt to demoralize society. That's a fact of life, and it exists because we live in a fallen, sinful world. Where immorality exists as vices and not violations of the non-aggression principle, society still has the opportunity to use the market to persuade and provide social services to reduce the incidence of immoral cultural vices.

There is also ample evidence that the benefits of the economic policies that libertarians favor create societies in which individuals seek to serve one another through the market, thereby enriching one another and creating greater prosperity for all. More open and economically liberal societies create abundance both materially and spiritually.

This isn't to say that society will be cured of its cultural ills. That won't happen until Christ returns. But the free market and libertarian legal order gives us the greatest opportunity to deal peacefully, creatively, and compassionately with these issues.

48. Do libertarians support the right to kill oneself?

The right to kill oneself is rooted in self-ownership and the right to do with our bodies what we want. This is not to say that we (libertarian Christians) see suicide as moral, desirable, or a social good. As Christians, we affirm that killing oneself is sinful (Ex 20:13). Again, it's helpful to look beyond the act to the social ills contributing to one's desire for suicide. By treating suicide as a health issue to be solved by the free market, solutions present themselves that may actually dissuade an individual from suicide and help them get onto a path of flourishing in life. Isn't that what we want? By contrast, punishing a person for attempting suicide only reinforces in their mind the utter despair and hopelessness in which they suffer. In fact, our criminal justice system magnifies this despair and hopelessness.

Another issue related to this is doctor-assisted suicide. Again, we would set aside the moral conundrum—because it is a conundrum (the movie *Me Before You* offers a sense of the moral conundrum). Sometimes it's a little too easy for Christians to offer up platitudes of God's plan and purpose. Tell that to a person who's suffered their whole life and struggled with the idea that God's plan was to bring them into the world to torture them. Though we would disagree with this caricature, it's definitely the wrong way to encourage a person in the depths of despair.

What libertarianism offers in this case is a free market with creative and innovative options to help those struggling to see the value of life, whether that despair be health related, job related, relationship related, or spiritually related. By allowing suicide to be legal, the idea is destigmatized in such a way that it's safe to talk about and safe to get help for. And, God forbid, should it happen, we can grieve it for what it should be grieved as—a tragedy, not a crime.

49. How can a libertarian expect a free society without a safety net to provide for the poor?

Christians have a personal obligation to look out for the poor, either through direct care or supporting those who provide direct care. In addition to this, libertarian Christians ask a broader question: how can we help those who are poor get to the point they are no longer poor or require others for support? This adds an important dimension to the "charity versus welfare" debate.

Many Christians against the welfare state claim that the Church and charitable individuals are charged with caring for the poor. Christians in favor of the welfare state claim that churches and charitable organizations cannot possibly meet the needs of all who are poor. Libertarian Christians point out that this is a false choice and that a third option is not only important but has proven to be effective: free markets with stable property rights for all individuals, regardless of social status.

In the end, libertarian Christians want to see a society where the need for charity and safety nets is nearly nonexistent because of the economic gains made by all in society. Only a free society with stable property rights can achieve this end.

50. How can a Christian fulfill Jesus' command to care for the poor in a free society?

When Jesus said in Matthew 26:11, "The poor you will always have with you," he was describing the kind of people his followers would be: ones who attracted the poor because of their love and care for them. Yet while Christians are to signal to the world that we are the community who loves and takes care of the poor, the signaling itself is not the purpose. The real purpose is to meet the needs of the poor.

We must resist the idea that the most poor are the only people who need our attention. Because there are varying levels of need and various types of poverty, we must be on the lookout for people we can help who are in need at whatever level. For example, the father who just got fired because of an addiction might not qualify in our minds as "very poor," but he and his family are in need.

Through personal responsibility, Christians can and should participate in or fund endeavors committed to the well-being of those on the margins. This well-being should not merely be about the charity of feeding empty stomachs or sheltering the homeless, but about the empowerment of human beings with untapped talents, skills, and something to offer their fellow human beings.

Care for the poor is often misunderstood as charity for those who lack, but a much broader vision of care is needed if we are to pursue human flourishing. We must seek to empower those on the margins because it is physically and spiritually nurturing to them.

Further Reading

The Abolition of Man | C.S. Lewis (Oxford University Press, 1943)

For the Least of These: A Biblical Answer to Poverty | Anne Bradley & Arthur Lindsley eds. (Zondervan, 2015)

When Helping Hurts | Steve Corbett and Brian Fikkert (Moody Publishers, 2014)

The War on Drugs is a War on Freedom | Laurence Vance (Vance Publications, 2012)

"Want to Win the War on Drugs? Portugal Might Have the Answer" | Naina Bajekal (Time, August 2018)

7

WHAT ABOUT PUBLIC GOODS AND SERVICES?

"Socialism, like the ancient ideas from which it springs, confuses the distinction between government and society. As a result of this, every time we object to a thing being done by government, the socialists conclude that we object to its being done at all."

— Frederic Bastiat

51. Without the state, who will build the roads?

While this question may at first seem like a trump card against the idea of privatization in general, it is readily answerable from both a theoretical and historical point of view. Simply put, roads would be produced both by companies and individuals. Their operations would be funded by tolls (for highways), subscription fees (for local roads), and neighborhood dues (for streets like those in front of your house). Throughout history, roads have been built privately and even continue to be built this way today. Most roads are not actually produced by the state but by private companies as contractors. The libertarian argument is to suggest that this should be expanded even further and not have the state involved in the first place.

52. Wouldn't it be inefficient for all roads to be tolled?

Even if all roads were privatized, not all roads would be toll roads. Your neighborhood probably would rather not operate that kind of system even if it were a gated community. Businesses desire people to frequent their establishments and therefore may invest in the road system around them in order to make it more appealing to go there. But ultimately, it is up to entrepreneurs to experiment and find ways to serve their road-going customers most effectively.

We could turn this question and ask if government-run road operations are efficient, safe, and cost-effective? Our experience in the United States, at least, suggests that such qualities are near non-existent on government roads. Think about it: if any business had to answer for nearly 40,000 people per year dying while using their goods or services, they'd probably be out of business in two seconds flat. Yet that is the reality of government roads. It's high time to get rid of road socialism.

53. Who will educate our children?

We are conditioned to believe that systematizing education is the best way to have a well-functioning social order. Yet education is as old as human existence, whereas schooling as we know it is relatively new. Once we understand this distinction, we can begin to imagine new ways of educating.

The question isn't really about who owns and operates the school system. Rather, it is whether we even *need* a formal system or if (just as in any market) it makes more sense to allow providers of education to innovate to meet the needs of their community and achieve an even greater outcome. For libertarian Christians, the idea that a central organization should dictate how, when, what, and where children should learn is unimaginative at best and abusive at worst. We can and should seek better educational opportunities for our children.

Here are a few ways in which education is made possible without a centralized public school system:

1. Starting a school funded by donations from those who have extra to give.
2. Independent teachers offering classes, either for a fee or funded by donation.
3. Private gyms and fitness studios offering Physical Education classes.
4. Starting a business that provides apprenticeships in exchange for inexpensive labor.
5. Parents schooling their own children or collaborating with other parents to do so.
6. Working in the political system to work toward a less institutionalized approach to education.

Those who follow Jesus should be pushing the way forward that helps those in need, by whatever peaceful means necessary.

Even if one argues that the state should provide a backup solution for children who "fall through the cracks," it does not make much sense that the funding and provision of education are run by the same institution. No other government safety nets are operated this way. Why should it be this way with education?

54. Who will protect children from child abuse? Who will rescue abused children?

The remedy offered to us today are Child Protective Services departments provided for by the state. These services rely on concerned citizens calling in to report suspected abuse. The problem with these services, as they exist, is that they're monopolized through the state. This has resulted in rampant abuse within CPS departments and foster care systems. One need only search Google to find endless reports of CPS failures, corruption of power, and foster abuse to see there's a problem.

This is no solution to child abuse! Children deserve better, and free market services could vastly improve responses to child abuse. And in fact, there are already some market choices available including Safe Families and Bethany Christian Services. These organizations provide services to troubled families and families in crisis. And being left to the free market and the natural regulation of the consumer, abuse within these protective services would be mitigated.

55. Who will catch the criminals?

It can be hard for some people to imagine anyone other than government being responsible for protecting us from criminals. "Crime" is something defined in modern society by the laws that state institutions have crafted, and it seems natural that state institutions would enforce these laws. In a libertarian society, there would be far fewer crimes and far fewer criminals by definition. Legal writers use two Latin phrases to distinguish between categories of crimes: criminal acts that are evil in themselves (*malum in se*) and acts that are crimes purely because the state has chosen to legally prohibit them (*malum prohibitum*). Libertarians generally reject the proposition that *malum prohibitum* crimes should be crimes at all.

That still leaves *malum in se* crimes to deal with. Generally speaking, everyone wishes to avoid being murdered, being the victim of theft, and so on. There is a strong demand in society for security services. The principal argument for public police forces is based on the idea that public safety is a "public good" that is not efficiently produced by markets.

Historically, public police forces have been created to carry out a number of different functions: keeping public order, controlling crime, performing various public safety services, and suppressing and controlling of undesirables. Government police forces win support within government because they reliably enforce the will of the sovereign, and they win business support because they socialize some of the cost of private security. Some of the origins of police in America are undeniably sinister. From the colonial period until the Civil War, slavers expended substantial resources in catching runaway slaves. The creation of the earliest government-funded police forces in Southern and mid-Atlantic American colonies circa the 1700s, largely revolved around socializing these costs of maintaining slave patrols.

Libertarians have a lot of different ideas about how security services would be provided in a libertarian society. One belief is shared by almost all libertarians: private companies should be doing a lot more, and government police would be doing a lot less.

56. Who will regulate air traffic or prevent future terrorist attacks?

Having government agencies like the Federal Aviation Administration (FAA) in charge of airplane safety and maintenance and the Transportation Security Administration (TSA) in charge of security at airports might make some people feel safer. Libertarians believe that private firms would be more successful than government bureaucracies at stopping dangerous cargo—and more efficient, too. It is not clear that the TSA is very good at what it does. Penetration testing of TSA security measures has shown that these measures are highly porous. While it is possible that these measures have deterred some bad acts, there is clearly much room for improvement in airport security. Many passengers pay extra for pre-screening credentials, suggesting that there is demand for more efficient, less burdensome security screening measures.

Crashing planes into each other is just as horrifying a prospect as losing them in a terrorist attack. Coordination of aircraft across space and time is essential for avoiding such a calamity. But there is no reason that this coordination must be done by the state. In 1996 in Canada, air traffic control was privatized and placed in the hands of profit-making enterprises instead of a public bureaucracy. Canada's private system is now recognized as one of the best in the world by industry watchdogs, and a model for other nations to imitate.

It is also important to remember that passengers are not the only people with a stake in safe air travel. Airplanes are expensive machines. Losing an airplane is expensive and disruptive to an airline, and the reputational costs of a deadly disaster can be even more damaging. Even if the FAA and TSA ceased operation tomorrow, airlines, their insurers, and their customers would all have a strong interest in making air travel safe. There are already airports operating today with private security screening, but they must use TSA protocols and TSA-approved equipment. Instead of a government bureaucracy providing a one-size-fits-all solution, libertarians promote competition in security services.

57. Some libertarians say public safety should be handled by insurance companies. What about people who aren't policyholders?

Many libertarians believe that insurance companies should play an even more important part in providing for security and dispute resolution services than they do today. But what about the uninsured? The good news is that insured and uninsured people have many interests in common. For example, my insurance company has a strong interest in fires on neighboring properties being extinguished quickly. If fires are allowed to spread, insurance companies will receive more claims and pay out more money. If fires are quickly extinguished, insurance companies will not receive these claims and will enjoy higher profits.

Even today, in a world where fire departments are heavily funded with tax dollars, insurance companies voluntarily expend many millions of dollars both directly and through grant-making foundations (including the Allstate Foundation, the State Farm Insurance Grant Program, and the Fireman's Fund Heritage in Action Program), to support fire departments of all sizes across the United States. While companies typically distribute grant money to areas where they market insurance products, most residents in the areas benefiting from these grants are not actually customers of the individual company offering the grant.

Libertarian writer Gil Guillory is one of the leading scholars on the feasibility of a subscription-based patrol and restitution service. In his work, he calculated that he would only need to sign up a tiny fraction of the residents in a subdivision to profitably patrol the entire area, reducing the incidence of crime for policyholders and non-policyholders alike.

Privatization of public safety functions does not disadvantage those who cannot pay or choose not to pay for these services. Many people would benefit from the free functioning of a private market for public safety services without paying any fee at all.

58. How would parks exist if not for the state?

It might initially seem like the state is necessary to protect certain kinds of natural resources, but how can we expect a government that mismanages practically everything to maintain a complex ecosystem? We can observe from the history of state-managed ecology projects that the government is far better at destroying than preserving. Besides, private parks already exist in various forms. From small private campsites to massive amusement parks (hey, they call them parks for a reason!), we can see that private ownership of land and the freedom to use it in entrepreneurial ways can surely allow for the development of the equivalent of any "government" park. Some parks, like Bryant Park in New York City, will be open to the public and run by private foundations, funded by donations from individuals and businesses. Some will be attached to businesses to encourage people to become customers of that business and to serve the community. Some will have subscription services or entry fees like a country club. The state is simply not necessary to ensure that parks stay solvent and operational.

59. What about people who can't afford to pay for these privatized services?

The beautiful thing about the free market is that competition tends to drive down prices of goods and services—especially those considered essential. State management, in contrast, trends exactly the opposite.

Take roads, for example. We would expect that competition amongst road producers would ultimately drive prices downward or even have multiple pricing tiers for different sections of the road. Nonetheless, there will likely be many options available for lower income individuals, especially as more competition arises in public transportation (since cities would no longer monopolize those services). We need to keep in mind that the government effectively has a legalized monopoly position on the roads of greatest concern here. Opening up competition eliminates that monopoly and allows more options at lower cost.

Besides driving costs down, free markets also drive prosperity through production. With greater prosperity, widespread poverty inevitably decreases in turn. Availability of services becomes less and less of an issue. Greater prosperity will also lead to greater charity activity. We already see private charity stepping up to fill the voids because of government mismanagement. There may always be those less fortunate who need help, but the state is not the best solution.

60. What about libraries?

Libraries were initially created because books were scarce and expensive. A wonderful aspect of our modern era is that books are far more plentiful and inexpensive than in the past. The advent of the internet age has changed the nature of the modern library, and the availability of information is greater than ever before in the history of the world.

Yes, libraries are wonderful, but they do not need to be funded by forced taxation. Of course, communities can still come together and create lending libraries that will look just like what occurs today. Perhaps they will have subscription fees, perhaps not, but we can be certain that books are not going away. In fact, people are doing this in a decentralized fashion right now through the "Little Free Library" movement. So don't worry; libertarians love books and love the dissemination of knowledge. We believe free people are able to organize efforts to spread knowledge in a multitude of effective ways, and do so better than the state, voluntarily.

Further Reading

The Privatization of Roads and Highways | Walter Block (Mises Institute, 2009)

Failure: the Federal Miseducation of America's Children | Vicki E. Alger (Independent Institute, 2016)

Order Without Law: How Neighbors Settle Disputes | Robert Ellickson (Harvard University Press, 1994)

To Serve and Protect: Privatization and Community in Criminal Justice | Bruce L. Benson (Independent Institute, 1998)

Land Use without Zoning | Bernard H. Siegan (Mercatus, 2020)

8

WHAT ABOUT NATIONALISM, NATION STATE, AND PATRIOTISM?

Babylon's futility is her idolatry – her boast of… moral ultimacy in her destiny, her reputation, her capabilities, her authority, her glory as a nation. The moral pretenses of Imperial Rome, the millennial claims of Nazism, the arrogant arrogance of Marxist dogma, the anxious insistence that America be "number one" among nations are all versions of Babylon's idolatry. All share in this grandiose view of the nation by which the principality assumes the place of God in the world.

–William Stringfellow

Real patriotism is a willingness to challenge the government when it's wrong.

–Ron Paul

61. Don't we need a common defense?

Individuals have a right to protect themselves from violence, and, thus, groups of people have the right to do so as well. But that doesn't mean every person everywhere needs the backing of a military from their native country.

The United States was never supposed to have a standing army, and plenty of countries do fine without them. In fact, more than twenty countries, such as Andorra and Liechtenstein, currently have no nationalized military apparatus at all. Acting from a position of neutrality often prevents antagonizing relationships from developing in the first place. Recall that Thomas Jefferson said in his first inaugural address, "Peace, commerce, and honest friendship with all nations... entangling alliances with none." Countries would do well to remember that free trade and friendship with others is far preferable to war. Libertarians often say, "When goods and services do not cross country borders, armies eventually will."

62. Don't countries have the right to self-determination?

Countries have a right to self-determination, the ability to choose their own destiny independent of other countries, inasmuch as the individuals do that make it up.

Self-determination for the individual is, essentially, a slightly different way of stating the non-aggression principle. Individuals have the right to do as they will, assuming that they do not commit aggression in their activities. Likewise, groups of individuals (such as a country) can act together, so long as they don't commit aggression. Remember, an action that is considered sinful, violent, or repugnant for an individual does not suddenly change its status if it is tacitly permitted by a group of people.

63. Shouldn't Christians be thankful we live in a free country?

Christians have been transformed by Christ, according to 1 Thessalonians 5:18, to be thankful in "all circumstances." That would certainly include where you reside! But thankfulness for your homeland and the good qualities it has does not mean you cannot or should not criticize its culture, behavior, and especially its state apparatus. We can respect the ways in which the United States has maintained liberty while simultaneously saying that the state is at odds with crucial liberty principles. The ways in which the state ever promotes liberty, in fact, are incidental and not fundamental to its being, since the state's existence is predicated on the threat of violence in the first place.

64. Can a Christian serve in the military?

Just like any major decision, we should always take into account all of the factors and weigh the benefits and costs. A Christian who joins the military should not only weigh the benefits to joining (to themselves, to the military, and to the nation it serves), but also the personal and wider costs associated.

When considering a moral choice of such importance, most of the considerations are imbalanced. For example, a young person considering joining would look at the skill development, leadership training, mind-body improvements, and educational opportunities afforded them by joining. The trade-offs might only be considered in comparison to what they are giving up: traditional college, private employment, extended time away from loved ones, the possible compromise of one's morals through the obligation to follow orders, traumatic physical and mental injury such as PTSD, and potentially losing one's life.

As disciples of Jesus, Christians are obligated to consider far weightier things in their decisions. Does this path obligate me to kill another human being because I'm commanded to? Does this path build character qualities that run counter to Christian values? Does this choice make it impossible for me to conscientiously object to acts I am commanded to do that go against the love of Christ? Will I be participating in an institution that thrives on loss of life and profits on conflict and war? Does this life choice compromise my duty to "love my neighbor as myself"?

With few exceptions, libertarian Christians believe that serving in the military obligates the Christian to unquestionably obey orders, some of which may command actions that run contrary to the principles of the Kingdom of God. Remember that first-century Roman soldiers who converted to Christianity often left their military positions because they could no longer morally justify what they did. The call to eschew violence then was too strong, and their example should still inform us today.

So what would be the exception? It's tough to say, but perhaps if there were an active and present threat to the wellbeing of our fellow citizens, it might be acceptable to join the military in order to help stop the aggression. Even in these circumstances, however, Christians can do many other things other than participate in war to protect, serve, and love their neighbors. At the very least, abstaining from promoting and cheering "our side" of a war conflict should be the first step in showing Christian love to one's neighbor.

It should be noted that two co-authors of this book, Kerry and Dick, have served in the U.S. military and fully agree with the above statement.

65. Shouldn't Christians honor those who sacrifice their lives for their countrymen?

Jesus said to his disciples that "No one has greater love than this, to lay down one's life for one's friends" (John 15:13). Clearly dying on behalf of others, as Christ did for the world, indicates the greatest kind of love one could have for another.

Many American Christians attribute these attributes to those who join a branch of the military. Those individuals who join, it is supposed, believe they are defending the freedoms of their loved ones and of strangers. In short, they are willing to die on behalf of others.

However, simply because a soldier dies while on active duty does not mean they died *on behalf* of their countrymen. To truly know this, we must understand why the soldier is fighting, not why he *thinks* he's fighting. Dying in combat for the operations of the United States military has rarely meant sacrificing on behalf of fellow countrymen (though that's how the state markets it), but it always means participating in acts of aggression against others.

We should commend any individual willing to make life-changing decisions that indicate sacrifice. In fact, we should all want to become people who are known for willingness to lay down our life for others (or other sacrificial endeavors less severe). But joining the military as a signal of one's willingness to sacrifice is but one way to indicate a character quality worth celebrating. Not only are there other ways to do this, serving in the military brings with it other conflicts for the Christian.

Further Reading

Swords into Plowshares: A Life in Wartime and a Future of Peace and Prosperity | Ron Paul (Ron Paul Institute for Peace and Prosperity, 2015)

The Myth of a Christian Nation: How the Quest for Political Power Is Destroying the Church | Gregory Boyd (Zondervan, 2007)

War, Christianity, and the State: Essays on the Follies of Christian Militarism | Laurence Vance (Vance Publications, 2013)

Farewell to Mars | Brian Zahnd (David C. Cook, 2014)

It Is Not Lawful for Me to Fight: Early Christian Attitudes toward War, Violence, and the State | Jean-Michel Hornus (Wipf & Stock, 2009)

The Early Christian Attitude to War | Cecil John Cadoux (1919)

A Century of War | John V. Denson (Mises Institute, 2017)

9

WHAT ABOUT SOCIAL JUSTICE?

"Like so much that is done in the quest for cosmic justice, it makes observers feel better about themselves – and provides no incentives for those observers to scrutinize the consequences of their actions on the ostensible beneficiaries. As in other cases, human beings are sacrificed to the tyranny of visions because those sacrificed are not the same as those exhilarated by the vision."

—Thomas Sowell

66. Shouldn't human flourishing be the goal of good government?

Human flourishing should be the goal of any human-based institution, both private and public, so long as it is done within its sphere of capacity and ability.

Christians who believe the state should guide or lead us to human flourishing usually have in mind initiatives and programs that force individuals and businesses to behave in certain ways they view as conducive to human flourishing. Yet they fail to recognize that governments are particularly bad at guiding free human beings in ways that yield certain results. When governments try to pick winners and losers through subsidies and special privileges, they almost always fail.

As an institution on the monopoly of violence in society, the state's narrow role should be to enable human flourishing through means that actually achieve human flourishing. That is, if the state's role is to protect private property by enabling free exchange, not only would the economy grow, individuals and communities would flourish not because of the state but because the state was in its proper role in society.

67. Private charity can't cover everyone's needs, so don't we need government?

Most people compare what the government spends on welfare for the poor to the private charity dollars spent on the poor, arriving at the conclusion that private charity organizations could not bear the burden of providing for the poor if the welfare state were simply removed. However, this comparison is unfair for two reasons. First, it does not account for the fact that private charity organizations, on average, have far less bureaucratic overhead than government-run ones. Money spent through private charities is often more effective than government-run welfare programs.

Second, and more importantly, it ignores a third but very prominent anti-poverty measure that doesn't require government at all: free market capitalism. People achieved prosperity in the past 200 years not through welfare programs but through free markets. Oftentimes, governments have regulated the market in such a way that it creates the conditions for higher unemployment, increased prices for goods and services, and other factors that burden the poor.

Charity is only a short-term solution to the direct symptoms of poverty, not its causes. A robust society addresses the root problems to poverty by looking at a variety of issues.

Libertarian Christians believe that because work is essential to our life and our well-being, being recipients of the fruit of other people's labor (whether private or public) can only go so far. What those in poverty want and need is the fruit of their own labor.

68. Didn't Jesus care about the poor? Isn't that really what social justice is all about?

Of course Jesus cared deeply about the poor. When he said, "the poor you will always have with you," it was a character marker of the type of people who were attracted to Jesus and his followers: those who were impoverished. So when we apply this characteristic of Christlikeness broadly to society, it is easy to believe that social justice is all about caring for the poor.

Yet social justice should consider a set of conditions, not a particular set of outcomes. Too often we evaluate the state of justice based on perceived outcomes without assessing the institutions that produce those outcomes. For example, those who lament wealth inequality rarely decry the central banking system which creates vast inequalities of both opportunity and government privilege. Because they are formed by human beings, institutions are also flawed and in regular need of reform. Social justice requires us to think about what is properly "social" as well as what is "just." The poor are far better served when they are treated as legal equals in a society rather than persons to be pitied. Christians should demand equal treatment under the law, freedom of enterprise, secure private property rights, access to adequate defense, expedient justice in courts, and a host of other institutional arrangements under which conditions the poor can flourish along with the rest of society.

69. In Acts, the early church shared all things in common. Wouldn't this be a good model for society?

The early church community in Acts is an example of what can happen when people voluntarily come together for a common purpose and mission. However, this should not make us want to emulate the scenario without first asking ourselves helpful and important questions. What conditions and cultural situations made it possible for them to succeed? Was this done out of necessity, survival, or prudence? Was this a common practice among other sects? How large was the community, and how did that contribute to its success?

When we step back and ask why something "works" in the Bible, we must take into account questions like the ones above. A few key observations should warrant skepticism toward applying this scenario to an entire modern economy:

1. All who belonged chose to belong, and nobody was forced to participate.
2. Their community was neither large-scale nor a nation-state.
3. Its participants were committed to the same mission; they were not a pluralistic society.

It is natural for humans to want to belong to a community that makes us feel like one big happy family. This is why many Christians pine after socialism: it feels really good. But as such situations scale to include larger numbers of individuals, that cozy feeling of belonging dissipates, the voluntary nature disappears, and a different sort of socio-political context emerges.

70. How should we then think about global and social issues such as immigration, racism/sexism, or the environment?

Libertarian Christians affirm that as divine image-bearers, humans are assigned to be stewards of the creation as well as to be socially mindful about the people around us. We also believe that sin has infected creation and that God is actively at work in restoring creation and human relationships to their original goodness.

This means we ought to think seriously about policies that restrict the free movement of free peoples (we treat this in detail in Chapter 10).

Racism is the ugliest form of collectivism, where an individual is judged and interacted with based not on their individual unique qualities, but on what they are perceived to be like based on their skin color or other physical features. Christian libertarians should always advocate for peaceful ways to eradicate racism, as well as the similar problem of sexism. Both are pernicious, and while they are far less prevalent in developed societies today, there are latent attitudes and subtle behaviors that should always be called out.

Creation care is concerned with good stewardship of the environment. When God gave humans dominion over the created world, it was neither a "do what you want" *carte blanche* nor a "don't leave any impact whatsoever" prohibition. Good stewardship requires wisdom and discernment, considers the short- and long-term effects of human action, and evaluates the trade-offs of decisions in order to promote human flourishing (see Chapter 12).

Further Reading

Was Jesus a Socialist? | Lawrence W. Reed (Intercollegiate Studies Institute, 2020)

Christian Faith and Social Justice: Five Views | Vic McCracken, ed. (Blooomsbury Academic, 2014)

The Quest for Cosmic Justice | Thomas Sowell (Free Press, 2002)

A Conflict of Visions: Ideological Origins of Political Struggles | Thomas Sowell (Basic Books, 2007)

"Don't Let the Left (and the Right) Steal 'Social Justice'" | Jamin Hübner (2019)

"Progressives, Libertarians, and God's Economy" | Doug Stuart (2015)

When All Else Fails: The Ethics of Resistance to State Injustice | Jason Brennan (Princeton University Press, 2018)

10
WHAT ABOUT IMMIGRATION?

"When innocent people seek to interact with willing others in ways that are productive and mutually beneficial, justice does not ordinarily allow other people to set up barriers between them."
— Jason Brennan & Bas Van Der Vossen

71. What does the Bible have to say about immigration?

The Bible tells immigrant story after immigrant story: Adam and Eve were exiled from the Garden of Eden, made refugees by their own sin. Joseph was the victim of fraternal violence and was sold into bondage in the strange land of Egypt. Israel made its exodus from Egypt to the then-unfamiliar Promised Land. Ruth was a foreigner who immigrated to Israel. Christ traveled in foreign lands as an infant fleeing for safety from Herod the Great's Massacre of the Innocents. Our savior identified with the immigrant, and he included the "stranger" as one of the groups whom he called the "least of these" (Matt. 25:34–46).

Scripture speaks clearly on the topic of how God's faithful are to treat immigrants. The Bible tells us that foreigners who come to our country must be afforded equal legal rights to people who are native-born (Ex. 12:49, Lev. 24:22). More than that, we are to love them as we love ourselves (Lev. 19:33–34). Immigrants are a segment of the community who are worthy objects of our charity (Deut. 10:14–22). Indeed, it is an outward mark of a righteous man that his door is "always open to the traveler" (Job 31:32). Israel was reminded by God of its heritage as a people who were once strangers in a strange land, and instructed that it would be hypocritical for them to mistreat the alien (Deut. 24:19–22). God warns of judgment for those who "deprive aliens of justice" (Mal. 3:5, Deut. 27:19). Widespread mistreatment of immigrants can lead to national judgment (Ezek. 22:7, 29–31, Jer. 22:3–5). Treating immigrants justly was one of the conditions for Israel's continuing to enjoy the blessings of the Promised Land (Jer. 7:6–7).

72. Didn't God establish nations to keep people separate?

The "nations" described in the Bible were not nation-states in the modern sense, but rather extended family groups or tribes who shared a common language and culture. The original division of nations occurred early in post-deluge history. Nations are first mentioned in the Bible in Genesis 10, in a passage naming the first generations born after the great flood subsided: the offspring of Japheth, Ham, and Shem. Genesis 11 then focuses on the particular events that led to the division of the nations by language and physical distance. The efforts of a united humanity to construct a tower to their own glory ("let us make a name," v. 4) displeased God. God responded by confounding their language, leading them to abandon their construction project and to set off in different directions across "the face of all the Earth" (vv. 8–9).

The children of Israel were selected as a nation set apart as God's chosen people, and they were commanded to keep away from the corruption and idol worship of other nations. Even before that, the first great order of separation for Israel was an internal schism. Moses separated the wandering people of Israel into groups of faithful and reprobate before the Lord caused the earth to swallow up the followers of Korah, Dathan, and Abiram (Num. 16:23–35).

The good news is that national divisions that came about due to sin and corruption can be overcome by the grace of God. Foreigners who worshipped the one true God were to be welcomed by the nation of Israel (Isa. 56:1–8). In the Great Commission, Christ commanded his followers to go to all nations teaching his commands (Matt. 28:16–20). Peter preached that God had revealed to him that he "should not call any man common or unclean," and told his listeners about a faith that offered hope to God-fearing people of all nations (Acts 10:28, 35). National divisions are a consequence of sin. Everyone who repents and believes in Christ can join the eternal, holy nation of God (1 Pet. 2:9–10).

73. Even libertarians affirm property rights. Isn't a closed border the national analogue to personal property?

No. It is true that libertarians firmly believe in property rights. A property boundary marks where one owner's claim begins and another's ends. That boundary should only be enforceable if the owner really owns the tract of land within. That is where the analogy comparing government borders to private property breaks down. Government does not own all of the property within its borders. Though government-held lands are extensive in the United States, the majority of American ground is privately owned. Not all of these private owners agree about how to enforce the national borders, or even the idea that they should be enforced by government at all.

Libertarians would agree that a person should not trespass on another person's property. But unlawful immigrants usually are not trespassers. The vast majority (approximately two-thirds) of such immigrants enter their destination country legally and simply overstay their entry visa. This means that they do not enter by trespassing. Instead, they enter the country by the same means as any other traveler. These immigrants then rent apartments from willing landlords, obtain employment from eager employers, and buy goods from eager retailers. The accusation that they are trespassers is simply false. A person who moves from Mexico to Texas is no more a trespasser than a person who moves from Georgia to Texas, whether they have government approval or not.

Aggressive border enforcement encroaches on private property and disrupts the normal movement of labor and capital. It also creates dangerous black markets in transportation, housing, and employment. Even worse, restrictive immigration policies interfere with the performance of our Christian duty to be charitable to immigrants and to reach all nations with the good news of the Gospel.

74. Without tough border restrictions, how do we protect people from foreign threats?

There is a popular perception of constant danger at borders. Unfortunately, such dangers do exist, and they are largely a consequence of the immigration controls and the War on Drugs (see Question 43). The opportunity to conduct a lucrative arbitrage is a powerful motivator to break the law. Human traffickers and drug cartel hitmen are largely the creatures of government prohibition.

If border restrictions were to be lifted, dangers currently associated with international borders would largely evaporate as well. The current restrictions focus a great deal on smuggling of contraband. Without such distractions, the line between hostile invaders and peaceful travelers would be much easier to discern. Libertarians generally believe that there is a real need for security services both locally and regionally.

Many liberty-minded writers have discussed how markets might produce security services (some are mentioned in the "For Further Reading" list at the end of this chapter). As a practical question, there can be no doubt that private firms are capable of going to war. Global mercenary operations in the years following the war in Vietnam demonstrated that private firms are more efficient at ending short-term conflicts and stabilizing an area of operations than government forces. Many thousands of military contractors were used in American operations during the Iraq and Afghanistan wars. Private contractors made up as much as one-fifth of the total occupation force in Iraq.

75. Wouldn't allowing poor immigrant laborers into the country permit others to take advantage of their status as poor?

As Christians, we can and should be concerned about human labor exploitation, especially when the situation involves predatory behavior.

Allowing immigrants from a relatively poor country into a relatively wealthy country does not inherently exploit the situation of the poor. To know whether such behavior is happening, we need to assess relevant information, and we don't always have what we need. If an immigrant travels across the border to perform work, he is doing so because he is choosing his best known available opportunity for work. If he were restricted to his own country, he would have fewer options. It is an unjust situation for this poor person to be restricted from voluntarily offering his labor to a willing employer.

Some object that this situation is suboptimal, and they would be right. It would be nice if everybody had the skills to perform high-value labor and the employers had the profit margins to pay top-dollar wages. But the world we live in is one of limited knowledge that increases through discovery, and it is up to us to discover how to best cooperate and exchange within the parameters of peaceful, voluntary work.

Lastly, we ought to be very careful to not assume that we know what is better for the lives of immigrants than they do for themselves.

76. Shouldn't we abolish the welfare state before we allow open immigration?

Many who favor libertarian politics but oppose open immigration use the existence of a welfare system as a reason to not favor open immigration. Setting aside the reality that most non-natives are not eligible for most welfare benefits, the argument has emotional appeal. It seems unfair to give non-citizens benefits that citizens pay for through tax dollars and that may raise citizens' taxes. If you abolish the welfare state, these opponents say, they would favor open immigration. But even this acknowledges that open immigration is the default libertarian position, since their argument is to overcome the default with a justifiable restriction on human liberty.

Their position ignores that a restrictive border necessitates highway checkpoints, an immigration police state, warrantless searches of property, forcible separation of children and their parents, and a host of other egregious practices.

The reality is that most immigrants do not come to take advantage of the welfare state, nor is the federal government required to provide aid to foreigners. In fact, some economists have calculated that open immigration actually reduces the burden of the welfare state.

While this argument has some initial emotional appeal (and because Milton Friedman said it), this appears to be yet another ad hoc reason to oppose the free movement of people and deny them their right to flourish.

77. How would a mass number of immigrants effectively integrate into their new host country?

This question is predicated on two false beliefs: First, that open immigration would immediately result in mass immigration, a possible but not likely outcome. Second, that "effectively integrated" should be the goal of permitting more immigrants.

If the federal government were to open its borders tomorrow morning, there would likely be an initial influx of new immigrants, which would fairly quickly increase the costs of moving for those who weren't quite as quick to immigrate. Markets would adjust, and immigration would stabilize.

Whether or not those immigrants would effectively integrate into their new host country depends on a lot of variables. While immigrants themselves sometimes struggle to adapt to their new society beyond survival, their children often thrive, and third-generation immigrants are quite well-integrated into society. While the "how" is an important question, it seems that American culture has proven for centuries that it can handle the adjustment many immigrants bring.

78. Wouldn't allowing open borders create a "brain drain," where the able and intelligent in poor countries leave the poorest of the poor behind?

In reality, it is restrictive immigration policy that permits only the best from other nations that creates a "brain drain" where the least-productive workers are left behind in their native country to survive. In an open borders situation, the poorest would be permitted to immigrate, and would be better off.

Many critics of open immigration are concerned that the GDP of the sending countries would reduce, creating a spiral of even more poverty. But this way of thinking only considers countries, and we should be thinking about *people*.

Aside from the moral problem of treating the wealthy more favorably than the poor, forbidding poor people in other countries from migrating essentially keeps them from making choices that they believe would improve their lives while cooperating with others in a broader economy. Additionally, poor people are often poor because they lack the opportunity to become more skilled and therefore relatively wealthier. The best example of open immigration benefiting not only the immigrants but the receiving areas is the expansion of the United States westward. Not only were free people able to improve their lives and the areas to which they moved, they were free to avoid harsh and unsatisfactory regions because no state was forcing them to remain.

In short, free movement of labor enriches, not impoverishes.

Further Reading

"What the Bible Says About Immigrants" | Norman Horn (Libertarian Christian Institute, 2014)

Open Borders: The Science and Ethics of Immigration | Bryan Caplan and Zach Weinersmith (2019)

In Defense of Openness: Why Global Freedom is the Humane Solution to Global Poverty | Jason Brennan and Bas Van Der Vossen (Oxford University Press, 2018)

The Production of Security | Gustave de Molinari (Mises Institute, originally published 1849)

"The Private Production of Defense" | Hans-Hermann Hoppe (Journal of Libertarian Studies, Vol. 14, No. 1, 1999)

11

WHAT ABOUT ABORTION?

"Abortion on demand is the ultimate State tyranny; the State simply declares that certain classes of human beings are not persons, and therefore not entitled to the protection of the law. The State protects the 'right' of some people to kill others, just as the courts protected the 'property rights' of slave masters in their slaves. Moreover, by this method the State achieves a goal common to all totalitarian regimes: it sets us against each other, so that our energies are spent in the struggle between State-created classes, rather than in freeing all individuals from the State."

- Ron Paul

79. Why are some libertarians pro-choice if abortion violates the non-aggression principle (NAP)?

Since libertarianism is predicated on the concept of self-ownership, many pro-choice libertarians believe that a right to abortion falls under a woman's bodily autonomy and so, in their view, does not violate the NAP. For them, human rights aren't expressed until some other stage (viability, birth, etc.). Though libertarianism recognizes human rights in terms of property rights, the ongoing debate relevant to abortion concerns when those rights begin.

Various figures throughout history have offered different answers. But even among pro-choice libertarians, this is still a contested point. Some simply hold to the feminist view of abortion, which says that even if the fetus has some measure of rights, no one has the right to live unbidden on another, and that includes the fetus. In this view, a fetus has human rights but doesn't have an inherent right to live, unwanted, in their mother's womb.

Another view, known as Evictionism, argues that the mother (like any other property owner) is legally permitted to evict, not kill, her unwanted fetus. Nuances of this position do permit lethal eviction (abortion) prior to viability. However, lethal eviction is impermissible where it's possible for the fetus to live outside the womb. So technological improvements, such as artificial womb technology, could conceivabley render abortion obsolete (and therefore legally prohibited) in the future. However, the Evictionist view is not the pro-choice argument for abortion. Many pro-choice libertarians disagree with Evictionism, arguing the state shouldn't have a legal interest in human life until after birth.

What this really shows is that the abortion debate is not a settled issue for libertarians, and it's our position that pro-life libertarians have a much stronger response to pro-choice libertarians than conservative pro-lifers.

80. Are there pro-life libertarians?

Yes! There are many pro-life libertarians, and one of the first groups to organize was Libertarians for Life, founded in 1976 by Doris Gordon. It began with Gordon, a non-theistic libertarian, citing various scientific and philosophical arguments for a right to life. Like pro-choice libertarians, most pro-life libertarians simply hold to their respective conventional view, often defending conventional arguments in libertarian terms. However, the evictionist position posits a third way—a distinctively libertarian take on abortion that warrants a distinctively pro-life response.

In response to Evictionism, LCI's Kerry Baldwin has been developing an alternative libertarian pro-life perspective. In Baldwin's view, the intractibility of the abortion debate is due to both sides compromising rights: pro-choicers compromise the rights of the fetus in favor of the woman, and pro-lifers compromise the rights of the woman in favor of the fetus. Similar to the Evictionist view, Baldwin makes an argument from the principle of self-ownership, using science to illuminate the facts of nature which support the argument that self-ownership begins upon completion of conception. She then argues against the pro-choice position that abortion is an act of self-defense because doing so violates the principle of proportionality—that is, abortion is a lethal response and is only justified if the fetus poses a corresponding lethal threat to the mother.

Her view takes into account not only the legality of abortion but also the problem of enforcement, and it asserts that an authoritarian enforcement of abortion is untenable in a truly just legal order. A just prohibition of abortion, she argues, requires both a libertarian legal system and a freed market that empowers women to make life-affirming choices.

81. Does being a libertarian mean I should be personally opposed to abortion but for legal abortion?

Criminalizing something involves two distinctions: (1) codifying the reason why it should be illegal, and (2) the manner of enforcement. What happens more often than not, especially in society today, is that we confuse these two distinctions. One can favor abortion prohibition and oppose certain forms of enforcement that are themselves unjust. In fact, the Christian libertarian view is that civil governance *may not* act unjustly even when attempting to exact justice.

A major element of the abortion debate (which Baldwin believes is the most divisive) deals with enforcement of abortion prohibition. For many pro-life libertarians, authoritarian enforcement of abortion prohibition proves to be draconian and therefore not a genuinely pro-life (or libertarian) alternative.

Concerns over draconian enforcement result in the ever growing number of "moderates" on both sides, who feel left with no other option than the "safe, legal, and rare" position. Other pro-lifers insist that abortion is morally outrageous enough to justify an authoritarian approach to enforcement. But it is the case with many issues concerning criminal justice that an authoritarian punitive system is unjust even for violent crimes that are already illicit.

So a libertarian pro-life position must take into account the criminal justice system as well. We are opposed to cruel and unusual punishment. The manner in which we deal with rights violators is a reflection of our views of the value of human life.

Libertarianism still involves many classical liberal principles that we take for granted: presumption of innocence, being secure in our persons and property, proof beyond a reasonable doubt, and others that necessarily exclude a number of current efforts to either incrementally decrease or abolish outright the practice of abortion.

Libertarians can rightly say something should be illegal, and even work towards legal prohibition of it, while also maintaining certain methods of enforcement and/or punishment should be in no ways permissible.

82. But wouldn't personhood laws enacted by the state protect unborn lives?

Who defines personhood?

The rights of the unborn should already be protected by the 14th Amendment to the U.S. Constitution. And yet, the Supreme

Court has determined that pre-viable fetuses do not qualify under the 14th Amendment.

There simply is not a good reason why "human" shouldn't equal "person." Every attempt to separate humanity from personhood results in privileged statuses, class warfare, racism, and eugenics. This is antithetical to a free (and libertarian) society. While philosophical debates over what constitutes personhood are intriguing and educational, no philosopher or philosophical system of thought has successfully separated personhood from humanity in a way that doesn't result in a draconian and dystopian view of society.

Does the state protect rights?

In fact, the *Roe v Wade* decision also determined that a woman's bodily autonomy is subject first to state interest. So her rights are not really protected, either. If the existence of the state means protecting human rights of both women and the unborn, then why aren't they doing it? Why are they acting contrary to the 14th Amendment?

The unfortunate reality is that personhood *has* been defined—and redefined—to fit particular agendas. And in an authoritarian system of government, especially one which has so monopolized power, we are left with a system that has no incentive to uphold already existing laws that don't serve state interest.

83. Wait a second, this is getting complicated! The problem of abortion is simple: it's sin and requires repentance. Why don't libertarian Christians just take this approach?

Conservative pro-lifers are also not settled on how to end abortion. This, unfortunately, causes a lot of infighting. One such approach is religious, and it's probably the more used since pro-lifers are often labeled religious fanatics. It can come in many forms, from street preaching in front of abortion clinics to forming ethical arguments based on Christian theology. Some even believe legal abortion is a "national sin" from which Americans need to repent. In their view, God withholds blessings from the church due to the legal status of abortion. The moral argument is not in dispute. Theological arguments, however, are.

So how can libertarian Christians respond to abortion without making a theological case?

God hasn't only revealed truth in scripture, or special revelation. He also has written truth into creation, or general revelation. Conviction of the truths of special revelation require the Holy Spirit. Conviction of the truths of general revelation require only persuasion.

We've already explained in previous questions how the libertarian principles of self-ownership and non-aggression are discovered in nature, and grounded in scripture. Since they're discovered in nature, non-Christians can be (and have been) persuaded that they are true. Abortion should be no different. God's general revelation through the natural and social sciences reinforces the moral truth about abortion. Taking the truths of general revelation into account, we find there are many more ways to end the practice of abortion than only calling for repentance or only changing the law.

We affirm the transformative work of the Holy Spirit through the preaching of the Gospel. We also affirm the call to Christians to live out the Gospel in a fallen world. This positively impacts the culture around us. Though we would never discourage street preaching or persuasion through theological arguments, we do remember the church has always lived in a fallen world.

The mission of pro-lifers should be the same regardless of the legal status of abortion. We are to always, "do justice, love mercy, and walk humbly with our God" (Mic 6:8). We are to act as free people by serving one another humbly and in love, not covering evil (Gal 5:13, 1 Pet 2:16). Because as Christians, we're called to "be imitators of God ... walk in love, just as Christ loved [us]" ... and doing so while we were yet sinners" (Eph 5:2, 8). And we are to leave vengeance of evil to God (Rom 12:19).

84. What should be done with women who have an abortion?

It's necessary for pro-lifers to maintain a consistent strategy on this question regardless of the legality. Our aim with abortion should always be to save lives and uphold legitimate rights.

In a society that permits abortion:

Many pro-lifers are led to believe that a society that legally permits abortion is a hopeless situation for the unborn, when really the hopelessness comes from the polarization of the topic and not the legality of it.

A free market is something pro-life and pro-choice libertarians strive for. In fact, it is likely the free market is more important to the pro-life cause than legal prohibition of abortion. Why? In a free market, pro-life and pro-choice services would compete, especially if the government has deregulated the industry (we know this sounds ominous, but bear with us).

Crisis pregnancy centers (CPCs) already compete with abortion clinics, and abortion clinics are largely subsidized. There are more CPCs now than abortion clinics, and CPCs provide more services to women with unwanted pregnancies than abortion clinics. The key to dealing with abortion where it's legally permissible is to be both innovative and persuasive. Providing better, less expensive, life-affirming options results in more women voluntarily making life-affirming choices (whatever those may be). And really, even in a society where abortion is legally prohibited, we still need women voluntarily making life-affirming choices.

This has less to do with amping up polemics and more to do with innovation and the specialization of labor. In a free market society, some people are motivated to prevent unwanted pregnancies, and some are motivated to provide life-affirming options when unwanted pregnancies occur. We need both of these aspects of the market! This would leave a relatively small percentage motivated to provide a dangerous, expensive, and immoral service, like abortion. There's a great deal that can be done with women seeking to free themselves from an unwanted pregnancy, so long as there is a free market.

In a society that does not permit abortion:

Here, too, the freed market is key, except the act of abortion would be illegal.

Unlike an authoritarian enforcement of abortion, a libertarian legal order is designed to provide restitution and recompense for crimes committed. This could be monetary restitution to a family member who has charged a woman with abortion. Or it could be a restorative justice model wherein the woman learns the impact of her decision on family, friends, and even society. Or perhaps she obtains services to help her avoid circumstances of an unwanted pregnancy in the future. The aim of libertarian civil justice is to avoid cruel and unusual punishment wherein restitution corresponds to the crime— even violent crimes like murder.

85. What should be done with doctors who perform abortions?

In a society that permits abortion:

Many people believe that where abortion is legally permissible, the majority of society will embrace it. But this isn't necessarily the case. Much of what drives a pro-abortion orientation of our health care system is bureaucratic regulation and licensing. If we consider this, one might see why pro-life incrementalism (regulating the abortion industry to limit access) is a tactic used by conventional pro-lifers. Both pro-lifers and pro-choicers fail to take into account the influence that bureaucratic regulation plays in promoting abortion. But a freed market, absent the regulations of bureaucratic agencies and legislators, wouldn't necessarily result in the abortion free-for-all that one might imagine. In fact, as of this writing, abortion rates have dropped to their lowest since Roe v. Wade.

Abortion providers would be subject to market forces just like any other service. Abortion alternatives would compete with abortion providers, and innovations would occur (on both sides) as a result. Both would also be subject to principles like "creative destruction," where the market finds less expensive, more effective alternatives that cause older options to "go out of business." While it's hard to say where the market would land on this, it seems that much of the polarization of the abortion issue stems directly from the politicization of it. Even by removing regulations without legally prohibiting abortion, libertarians would be allowing market forces to work. And if these market forces can do things like lift the entire world out of abject poverty (which is mutually beneficial for all), then it's likely market forces will promote life-affirming options to women with unwanted pregnancies, and abortion providers would become an archaic, cruel, and expensive service incompatible with a free society.

In a society that does not permit abortion:

Given that a freed market would likely push abortion out as an acceptable means of dealing with unwanted pregnancies, then abortion service providers would likely be much fewer than we would imagine now. Nonetheless, abortion isn't likely to be completely eliminated by the market. So, if we operated in a freed market society where abortion was legally prohibited, it's not difficult to imagine what would happen to abortion providers. They would be subject to the same sort of criminal justice system described in Question 84. We still wouldn't need an authoritarian legal system to deal with illicit abortion services.

86. What about the Supreme Court? Shouldn't that weigh heavily on my vote for a president because the Supreme Court can overturn Roe v Wade?

If you look at abortion cases heard by the Supreme Court from Roe v. Wade to the end of George W. Bush's Administration, Republican-appointed justices are responsible for *deciding* and *upholding* Roe v. Wade. There were at least two opportunities for Roe v Wade to be overturned: in 1989 with Webster v. Reproductive Health Services, and in 2002 when Republicans had control of all three branches of the federal government.

In 1989, the Court upheld a Missouri statute which created some restrictions through regulations of abortion and abortion providers. The statute's preamble included this statement, "the life of each human being begins at conception", and "unborn children have protectable interests in life, health, and well-being."

According to the ACLU, the US Solicitor General invited the Court to use this case to overturn Roe. Republican-appointed Justices William Rehnquist, Anthony Kennedy, Sandra Day O'Connor, and Antonin Scalia (all Republican-appointees) along with Democratic-appointed Justice Byron White, upheld Missouri's restrictions on abortion, but didn't overturn Roe.

In 2002, George W. Bush was president. Republicans gained a majority in both houses of Congress, and there was a majority of Republican-appointed justices on the Supreme Court. If all we needed was a Republican majority in all three branches of government to overturn Roe, 2002 was the year it should have happened. Instead, all we got was the Partial-Birth Abortion Ban Act which effectively reversed Sternberg vs Carhart, a previous Supreme Court decision, permitting partial-birth abortion.

But here's the worst of it: *Roe v Wade* will never be overturned! Doing so would damage the Court's reputation. This is according to their decision in *Planned Parenthood vs Casey*. Roe is less about abortion access for women, and more about the Court's dictating the boundaries of a woman's liberty interest concerning reproduction, while also regulating the abortion industry. And while Republicans give lip service to being staunch advocates of the unborn, the record shows that the Republican Party has no interest in overturning Roe v Wade.

87. Shouldn't I vote for a party or candidate that is pro-life? I just can't stomach voting for a pro-choice candidate!

What constitutes a pro-life party or candidate, though? As we see from Question 86, the party normally associated with being "pro-life," the Republican Party, isn't really out to end abortion. They may prefer heavily regulating it, but their interest is the same as that of the Supreme Court: to protect their reputation in the eyes of mainstream voters.

If we understand the abortion issue in three parts, then we can begin to see how pro-lifers might reconsider their vote:

1. The legal rights aspect
2. The legal enforcement aspect, and
3. The praxeological (or economic) aspect.

Libertarians have more common ground on abortion. Both pro-life libertarians and pro-choice libertarians agree on points two and three. And there is still an internal debate on point one, even among pro-choice libertarians.

However, pro-life Republicans only agree on point one, and disagree on points two and three. Pro-life Republicans can't even agree on how to move forward. Questions 82 and 83 above already explain why points two and three are so vital to the cause of ending the practice of abortion. In other words, even a pro-choice libertarian is more pro-life than a pro-life Republican.

For nearly half a century, pro-lifers have been trying to reverse history by reversing the decision of *Roe*. While this may have been feasible closer to the time of *Roe*, it's not feasible now. Too much has happened since.

The beauty of the libertarian approach to abortion is that, we agree on the practical application of legal enforcement and economics, even if we disagree on the legal rights aspect causing us to live in a legally pro-choice society. Pro-lifers can do more with that situation to end abortion than they can with a pro-life authoritarian party or candidate.

The pro-life libertarian view is not one of control, but one of empowerment of the individual. So yes, you can vote for personally pro-choice libertarian candidates because they will not be interested in regulating life-affirming options out of the freed market.

88. If you can be libertarian and pro-life, then why doesn't the Libertarian Party platform reflect that?

While we would distinguish between libertarian philosophy and the political platform of the Libertarian Party, we do believe the party could word the abortion plank differently. The aim of the party platform should reflect what the Party has consensus on, while recognizing the ongoing internal debate. The fact is, pro-choice and pro-life libertarians are unified on a lot more regarding abortion than non-libertarian factions are.

First, we all agree that tax dollars should not be used to subsidize abortion. A bedrock tenet of both the Party and libertarian philosophy is that taxation is theft, and governments should not be using it to subsidize anything, anyway, including abortion.

Second, both pro-life and pro-choice libertarians believe the free market is best equipped to provide options for women who aim to avoid unwanted and/or resolve crisis pregnancies. We also believe in the self-ownership of women (and therefore their bodily autonomy) that affords them the right to make decisions about their own bodies and reproductive goals.

Where we disagree is whether one of the plethora of options available to women should include abortion and whether self-ownership of the woman extends over the body of the fetus. Neither one of these disagreements should supersede our agreement that a free market economy and self-ownership are foundational to our views.

We argue that a consistent libertarian position on abortion doesn't compromise the rights of either the fetus or the woman. We still can work together with pro-choice libertarians toward the common goal of a free society, knowing that the logic and principles are on the side of the pro-life argument and that our friends will see the error of their position in time.

Further Reading

Challenge to Liberty: Coming to Grips with the Abortion Issue | Ron Paul (Ron Paul Enterprises, 1990)

Abortion: A Rational Look at An Emotional Issue | R.C. Sproul (Reformation Trust Publishing, 1990)

Libertarian Christian Perspectives: Abortion | Libertarian Christian Institute (www. libertarianchristians.com/abortion)

Mere Liberty: On Abortion | Kerry Baldwin (www.mereliberty.com/abortion)

12

WHAT ABOUT THE ENVIRONMENT & CREATION?

"Animals are forced to adjust themselves to the natural consequences of their environment; if they do not succeed in this process
of adjustment, they are wiped out. Man is the only animal that is
able—within definable limits—to adjust his environment purpo-
sively to suit him better."

—Ludwig von Mises

89. What does the Bible say about our responsibility to the earth's wellbeing?

God said in Genesis 1:28 to "Be fruitful and increase in number; fill the earth and subdue it." This is sometimes called the
"dominion mandate." God created the world "good" in all its
wonders, but it was also created to be built upon. We are given
many stories and parables in the Bible that describe cultivation
and caretaking of resources. The natural world in the beginning
is described as a garden. Gardens are meant to be worked, and
that work inherently means that the garden is incomplete. God's

intent from the beginning was for humanity to work the earth, discover it, improve it, and create value from it. That work is a partnership with the one who created it all.

Therefore, the destiny of the whole earth is not pure wildland, but cultivation by its inhabitants. We are those cultivators. Utilizing the earth's resources for economic activity is what we were intended to do. Now, that does not mean we should be utterly wasteful and foolish with those resources, but it also means we do not have the right to assume we know better than our neighbor how he can use those resources that he rightfully owns. We can cooperate and trade to be more efficient and effective in the consumption of resources. In fact, history bears out that private ownership and free trade actually improve the environment overall!

90. What is the best way to understand our relationship to the environment?

The natural environment and the resources in it are great blessings that have been entrusted to us. That same environment also presents us with challenges that we must overcome in order to survive. Since the Fall, mankind has lived in a state of natural poverty and decay (Rom. 8:18–21). Rather than the abundance and safety of the Garden of Eden, the fallen world constantly presents us with such dangers as starvation, exposure, and disease. In his mercy, God has provided people the tools that we need to face these challenges, starting with the first garments he fashioned for Adam and Eve from animal skins (Gen. 3:21). God told Adam then that life after sin would require hard work (Gen. 3:17–19, 23).

Though the world groans under the bonds of sin (Rom. 8:22), it was not created as a cruel obstacle course to torment sinners. In fact, everywhere we look we can see visible wonders that point us to the glory of God (Ps. 65:8). Abraham was the first to refer to God as the one who provides (Gen. 22:14). As we use the resources that God has seen fit to grant us, we should use them as mindful stewards of a divine blessing (Matt. 25:14–30). The righteous take care to leave something of value for future generations (Prov. 13:22).

91. How could a free society protect the environment?

A free society is one where property rights are respected. Property owners have a much stronger incentive than politicians to protect natural resources because preserving precious capital provides for future opportunities to profit (see Question 92).

When property boundaries are clear and unambiguous, neighbors can more readily hold each other accountable. If a neighbor begins emitting toxic materials into a waterway, people downstream whose property is damaged should have a legal right to seek damages. Too often, in a system where environmental regulation is provided through government, political decision making can lead to wasted resources. Under modern environmental regulatory regimes, polluters and other bad actors may even be able to defend their harmful actions legally by pointing to government licensure and compliance with relevant regulations.

In a free society, property owners would have a better chance at holding others accountable for the environmental damage that they cause. When environmental waste is priced into market behavior, market actors will seek to avoid that source of liability.

Finally, it is important to point out that governments do not just fail to protect the environment; in fact, they are among the worst polluters. A 2020 report concluded that the United States military is the "largest single institutional consumer of hydrocarbons in the world," and that American military spending artificially induces greater reliance on dirty fuel sources. As a society relies more on accountable market institutions and less on wasteful bureaucratic ones, it is reasonable to expect more careful environmental stewardship to result.

92. Doesn't the corporate drive for profit come at the expense of the environment?

Profit and preservation of resources are not necessarily at odds with each other. In fact, private property owners have a strong incentive to conserve their privately owned resources. Unfortunately, when government owns and manages natural resources, there is an incentive for private parties to attempt to get as much as they can until the resource is exhausted.

From time to time, we see news articles about a politician controversially opening up government-held lands to mineral extraction, logging, or some other potentially destructive private use. In these cases, the most basic incentive for conservation is missing: private ownership. It is rational to maximize profits, and for as long as human beings live in a fallen world with scarce resources, they will seek to do so.

If we wish to conserve natural resources, society must be ordered in a way that aligns the profit motive and self-interest with conservation. The most obvious reason that a forester would plant trees is that he expects someday to reap a benefit from that planting. Property rights are required for that expectation to make sense. Consumer preferences can drive even the largest companies to consciously work to reduce the negative environmental impacts of their enterprise, not because of government regulations, but because they want to be seen by consumers as environmentally responsible.

93. Even if we are improving the planet, what about adverse effects like pollution?

We must recognize that some pollution is inevitable simply because of entropy—energy consumed is never 100 percent efficient, and some wastage will occur in the form of emissions or lost heat.

The bigger concern, though, is hazardous waste. Is it possible that someone will pollute land? Yes, absolutely. And to the extent they own that land, then that is technically theirs to do with as they will. The moment, however, that they damage someone else with their pollutant, they are then liable for those damages in the form of a tort (a civil lawsuit). The polluter would have to pay restitution for those damages and restore the property (or health) of the claimant. But these people will be few, and those who act so foolishly will not own much.

Strong property rights and restitution end up protecting the environment far better than states ever do. Keep in mind as well that the top polluter in the United States is, ironically enough, the United States federal government.

94. Isn't something as global as climate change an issue that requires a global, collective solution? What is the free market solution to climate change?

Assuming that climate change is really happening and is anthropogenic in nature, a unilateral collective solution handed down from something like the United Nations is a bad idea.

First, the data looking back does not necessitate a forward look that is catastrophic. Models of the future are massively uncertain, and their predictions of global climates and the need to "fix" the predicted issues are dangerous at best and unjust to billions at worst. Forcing the world economy to use less energy not only will likely not have the intended effect but also will guarantee a tremendous loss of future economic growth that would benefit the impoverished across the world. A free market solution is to adhere to strong property rights and privatize transportation systems (see Questions 51-52).

In energy markets, nuclear power plants are without a doubt the most cost-effective and cleanest way to produce power, and governments that claim to care about the environment yet shackle nuclear energy with unending regulations are doing the world a terrible disservice. The most recent nuclear reactor to come online in the U.S. was installed in Tennessee - in 2016. The next most recent came online in 1996. Why is this? Regulatory burden. Ultimately, free markets are life-bringing ventures and restricting their operations by fiat will take that life away.

95. Since many in the world do not accept libertarianism, are there legitimate compromises that libertarians can make that would be considered good stewardship?

The first thing libertarians can do is to take personal responsibility for themselves and their businesses. It's a good thing, of course, not to litter and follow the general guidelines of their community with respect to waste disposal. Being mindful of appropriate reclamation of hazardous waste is essential. Libertarians should support the improvement of property rights laws as they pertain to pollution as well. Encourage efforts that move land and resources into private hands rather than the state. Remember, the environment's worst enemy is statism, not the free market.

Further Reading

Environmental Stewardship in the Judeo-Christian Tradition | Jay Richards and Robert Sirico (Acton Institute, 2007)

Energy: The Master Resource | Robert L. Bradley, Jr. and Richard W. Fulmer (Kendall Hunt Publishing, 2004)

"Property Rights vs. Environmental Ruin" | David Theroux (Independent Institute, 1994)

The Moral Case for Fossil Fuels | Alex Epstein (Portfolio, 2014)

"Law, Property Rights, and Air Pollution" | Murray N. Rothbard (Cato Journal, Vol. 2, No. 1, 1982)

"Can the Government Solve Transportation Pollution?" | Norman Horn (Ethics, Place, & Environment, Vol. 12, No. 2, 2009)

"Our Stewardship Mandate" | Robert A. Sirico (Acton Institute, 2010)

Nature Unbound: Bureaucracy vs. the Environment | Randy T. Simmons, Ryan M. Yonk, and Kenneth J. Sim (Independent Institute, 2016)

13

CHRISTIAN MISCONCEPTIONS
OF LIBERTARIANISM

"The one who first states a case seems right, until the other comes and cross-examines."

— Proverbs 18:17

96. Don't libertarians think greed and selfishness are virtues?

Certainly some libertarians are greedy and selfish—just like some political conservatives and progressives. But there is nothing about libertarian political theory that lauds such behaviors as good and right. On the contrary, libertarianism suggests that the nature of the aggressive political process is to attract those corrupt individuals who are indeed greedy and selfish to positions of power, where instead of having to satisfy others' needs to gain anything (as in the marketplace), they can use that power to steal what they want from others. While the marketplace rewards those who serve the needs of others through mutual exchange, politics incentivizes direct greed with its very structure.

However, you might also have heard of the "virtue of selfishness" as explained by Ayn Rand, whom many libertarians respect. Some of Rand's teachings are antithetical to Christian values, but it's notable that Rand's use of such language is meant to combat the oft-proclaimed mantra that the state is inherently altruistic and is "better" than the marketplace where everyone is always and only "greedy." Instead, Rand says that it is good to aspire, to achieve, to create, to act in one's self-interest. As Christians, we even believe it is in our own self-interest to seek after God because it is the end of man to glorify God and enjoy him forever! So, self-interest in the right perspective is a good thing (see Question 19).

97. Aren't libertarians hedonists who just want to live however they want to?

Libertarians don't promote libertinism (the total disregard of any form of authority or social convention); we're just about promoting liberty.

Libertarianism is not a full moral or aesthetic theory, but only a *political* theory, which is a subset of moral theory dealing with the proper role of violence in public life. Libertarianism suggests what the proper role of civil government is and how it should behave (if at all), since it claims for itself the power to coerce others with physical force. Ultimately, libertarians say that everyone should be free to do as they will so long as they do not initiate aggression against others. That may make it possible for people to live as a certain kind of hedonist (again, so long as they don't commit aggression), but libertarianism doesn't make a claim about every activity surrounding human life, much less condone hedonism.

With liberty, though, one is free to act upon their deeply held moral principles without fear of violent reprisal, and that includes the religious freedom that Christians have sought since the beginning of our shared faith.

98. Why do libertarians seem to think all people are good and don't need a state to control them?

On the contrary, libertarians don't assume people are good at all. James Madison wrote in the Federalist Papers, "If Men were angels, no government would be necessary." The libertarian takes this even further by saying that it is precisely because humans are not angels that a government founded on aggression should not exist. Humanity cannot be trusted with the reins of power as such, even if it is purportedly given "checks and balances."

Madison believed a state must first be "enable[d] to control the governed," and then "oblige it to control itself." But how is this to occur but for the same non-angelic people that we said could not govern themselves to begin with? The libertarian suggests that institutionalizing aggression in government is nonsensical because humanity is not inherently good enough to hold that power without corruption. No coercive government can be structurally set up to get around this; such is the nature of aggression and power.

99. Why do libertarians seem to reject the sinful nature of humanity?

Perhaps one can argue that because not all libertarians are Christians, these libertarians don't believe in the sinful nature of humanity in the first place, but it is the same for political conservatives and progressives as well.

As should be evident from the libertarian arguments against political power throughout this book, libertarians have a keen sense for the evil people can perpetrate against one another when social institutions are set up with aggression at their forefront. Libertarian historians take great pains to understand the depth of human depravity that takes place through states and their activities, especially wars and their effects on more common people. Libertarians don't reject the sinful nature of humanity, but rather pinpoint just how awful the sinful nature of people can come out when political power corrupts them even further.

An evil person acting alone is much more easily thwarted than an evil person commanding the power of the state.

100. Why do libertarians seem to have simple answers to complex problems?

Libertarians do not purport to know the answer to every possible problem that will crop up if we reduce the state's power in everyday life. However, libertarians will suggest that people acting with rational self-interest can organize themselves in many unexpected ways to solve increasingly complex problems. This is an entrepreneurial process where people will take risks, make cost-benefit analyses to see what works and what doesn't, and then seek to invest in the means to solve those problems for others and gain a benefit through mutual exchange (free trade). We cannot know ahead of time what the exact outcome will be.

If libertarians did have exact answers to everything, that would suggest that one should simply put libertarians in charge of the world and have them run every aspect of society — but that would be antithetical to libertarian philosophy.

101. Doesn't libertarianism reject morals and make decisions on cost-benefit analysis?

This is a similar question to whether libertarians are merely "hedonists" or not (Question 97) but with a twist. It is true that there are some people who believe that government activity should be based solely on a cost-benefit analysis of a policy, but libertarians don't measure policy like that. Libertarians believe in the natural rights of every individual in person and property, and these are inviolable. Therefore, libertarians don't reject moral intuitions at all, but rather arrive at their political principles based on a particular subset of moral principles applicable to public life.

The key is that libertarians believe that moral principles do not fall away if someone suddenly becomes elected to a government position or is born into a monarchy. Libertarians say that there is no privilege of position and every individual is held to the same moral principles. That sounds rather Christian, actually!

102. Is Libertarianism an all-encompassing worldview?

Absolutely not! Libertarianism is concerned with political theory, which is certainly part of a worldview. A worldview includes, but is not limited to, views on all aspects of life including cultural, social, linguistic, ethical, and economic, but libertarianism does not purport to be the answer to life, the universe, and everything. If anything, the fact that the two major parties *do* purport to answer all aspects of life is an erroneous extension of political theory outside its proper boundaries.

Libertarians are always more than libertarians, and the Christian libertarian especially has more to be concerned with than politics alone. We have a prior and more important commitment to serve Jesus Christ, to love and provide for our families, and to seek lasting personal fulfillment through useful work and relationships.

Understanding political theory is important, helping to inform various parts of our lives, but it is not everything. We cannot stress enough in this book that we agree with the message of the Gospel and the words of the Westminster Catechism that man's chief end is "to glorify God and enjoy him forever." Part of how we glorify God is by seeking truth in all aspects of life, and getting our political theory right helps ensure that we are proper neighbors and respecters of all mankind.

Further Reading

Can Christians Be Libertarian? (Norman Horn debates Al Mohler) | www.MoodyAudio.com

"Myth and Truth About Libertarianism" | Murray Rothbard (1979)

The Libertarian Theology of Freedom | Edmund A. Opitz (Hallberg Publishing Corporation, 1999)

The Soul of Atlas | Mark David Henderson (Reason Publishing, 2013)

BUT WHAT ABOUT...?

We wrote this book to provide succinct and clear answers to the most common questions we are asked as libertarian Christians. But we are not under an illusion that this short book says everything that needs to be said. There will always be more questions, and there will always be fresh ways to articulate answers to reach more people. New political circumstances, pandemics, scientific discoveries, and technological advancements often require us to speak differently about timeless truths, and we are prepared to adapt to reach more people.

In other words, this book is just the beginning of an ongoing conversation. We invite you to keep that conversation going by continuing to ask more questions and by inviting more people into it. That's why we've created www.faithseekingfreedom.com as a place to share this work with others, ask new questions, and dive into more resources to satisfy your curiosity. We welcome and appreciate all polite and civil responses, whether they are positive, negative, or a mixture of the two.

Welcome to the conversation! Please keep it going by joining us at www.faithseekingfreedom.com.

ACKNOWLEDGEMENTS

Projects of this scope are not done without a strong network of support, and the Libertarian Christian Institute could not accomplish all that it does every day without the encouragement and support of our readers, listeners, and donors.

We are very grateful to the powerhouse editing team at Bellwether Communications, Elise Daniel, Jacqueline Isaacs, and Morgan Feddes Satre. Their careful work made ours much improved.

To Mary Ruwart, whose book *Short Answers to the Tough Questions* inspired this work. Thank you for being a stalwart defender of individual liberty and encouraging us along the way with this project.

To Larry Reed, whose personality and warmth leave as much an impression on those who know him as his rigorous and tireless defense of freedom does on everyone else. We are honored by your enthusiastic support for the work of LCI and for writing the Foreword to this book.

To Erik Lindborg, who has faithfully helped keep this project in check and as on time as we could handle. Your stabilizing force in our organization has made this project a genuine success.

To Chris Williams, who gave us important feedback during the writing process, and whose company, Podsworth Media, produced the audio version of this book.

To our board members—Wade Beavers, Josh Feinberg, David Theroux, Nick Gausling, Katelyn Horn, Jason Rink, and Alexander McCobin—for walking with us along the journey and for being among our greatest advocates.

The authors each wish to acknowledge important people in their lives.

From Norman

There are too many people to thank in these few words, but I'll give it a fair shot. I'm grateful to my wife, my parents, and my in-laws for always being encouraging of these efforts, in their own unique ways. My dad (Gary) deserves a special shout-out for reading an early draft of the book and offering so many helpful comments. I am immensely thankful for the supporters of LibertarianChristians.com and now LCI over the years. Without you guys, there's no reason to write a book. And finally, I am blessed by the team we put together to make this book happen. We turned an idea into reality, my friends, and I am thrilled to see where it takes us next.

From Doug

Every author must recognize a debt owed to the many contributors to their own life, and my indebtedness stretches in many directions. To my parents, who taught me the value of hard work, the importance of seeking the Lord above all else, and who always permitted me to question things, even if it sometimes frustrated them greatly! For my entire life they've been the epitome of intentional love and forgiveness. To the influences in my theological journey who taught me the way of non-violence and how to read the Scriptures through the lens of the risen Christ: N.T. Wright, Tim Keller, Greg Boyd, Bryan Zahnd, Peter Enns, and many others. To my libertarian influences, who taught me to think beyond the false dichotomy of politics: Bob Murphy, Tom Woods, Larry Reed, Ron Paul, Andrew Napolitano, Steve Horwitz, Stephan Kinsella, Mike Maharrey, Jason Brennan, Kevin

Vallier, Art Carden, Bryan Caplan, Russ Roberts, and plenty more! To my libertarian comrade and co-conspirator, Norman Horn, without whom this journey to freedom would have been far less fun and rewarding. And most important to me, to my wife, who has championed my life pursuits sometimes a bit more than I have myself! My world is forever better with her, not only as a best friend and loyal life partner but also a witty, intelligent thinker who sharpens my sometimes sloppy thinking in the most loving way necessary.

From Kerry

I'll begin by thanking The Libertarian Christian Institute for giving me the opportunity to write for them. To my parents, Dave and Nina Baldwin, I'm thankful for all of the support they've given me, especially in the last few years. To my kids, Aiden, Saoirse, and Deaglan, who've had the unfortunate task of distinguishing the difference between their playing on the computer for hours and my working on the computer for hours. I'm proud of them as they've persevered through difficult times. To Gregory, for being a dear and faithful friend, who helped me understand the works of Mises, Rothbard, and others particularly through a Reformed theological perspective. Finally, I give thanks to God for blessing me so much and giving me the freedom to do what I love with wonderful people. I can attest to the fact that God does "supply every need according to his riches in glory in Christ Jesus" (Phil. 4:19). I pray the message of freedom will ring loudly once again and across the world and in the church, and I'm humbled by the opportunity to be one of many voices calling for it.

From Dick

My parents, Dick and Carolyn Clark, first told me about my sin, God's love, and the gift of salvation that Jesus Christ bought at Calvary. They taught me that this world is not our home, and that believers should never be afraid to stand on the solid foundation of God's word. I am forever indebted to Bob Murphy, who convinced me in 2001 that God's law is incompatible with statism. I am also grateful to many other tireless champions of liberty I first met in the Mises Institute orbit: Lew Rockwell, Jeff Tucker, John Sophocleus, Mark Thornton, Tom Woods, Walter Block, Robert Higgs, Guido Hulsmann, Joe Salerno, Roderick Long, Stephan Kinsella, Anthony Gregory, Manuel Lora, Robert Wicks, Daniel Coleman, Brian Martinez, and Gil Guillory. Finally, I must thank my beloved wife, Justina, who has been my indispensable framework, offering both encouragement and candid criticism when they were needed most.

ABOUT THE AUTHORS

Dr. Norman Horn is the founder and President of the Libertarian Christian Institute. He holds a Ph.D. in Chemical Engineering from the University of Texas at Austin and a Master of Arts in Theological Studies from the Austin Graduate School of Theology. He has won numerous awards for his writings and research in both engineering and theology, and has authored multiple peer-reviewed publications in natural sciences, economics, and political theory. He works as a professional chemical engineer, resides in Missouri with his wife and three children, and is an a cappella worship leader in the Churches of Christ. He has been a passionate defender of individual rights and libertarianism from a Christian perspective for over fifteen years.

Doug Stuart is CEO of the Libertarian Christian Institute. He holds an MDiv from Biblical Seminary, and his writing and speaking focus on challenging the status quo. Doug became a full-fledged libertarian because Christians can defend liberty as a necessary aspect of loving others and defending the rights of the oppressed. Doug currently lives with his wife and three children in Lancaster, PA, where he freelances as a graphic designer and video producer. He has served as a deacon at an evangelical church, where he has also taught classes on film and culture, evangelism, faith and economics, and non-violence.

Kerry Baldwin is an independent researcher and writer with a B.A. in Philosophy from Arizona State University. Her website is

MereLiberty.com and she focuses on libertarian philosophy and reformed theology. She challenges readers to rethink prevailing paradigms in politics, theology, and culture. She is a confessionally Reformed Christian orthodox Presbyterian in the tradition of J. Gresham Machen (1881–1937), an outspoken libertarian and defender of Christian orthodoxy. Kerry holds libertarian anarchism to be properly grounded in Reformed Christian convictions, and finds an alternative to patriarchialism, feminism, egalitarianism, and complementarianism in a Reformed perspective. Kerry is a single, homeschooling mother of three. She enjoys outdoor activities in the Jemez mountains near her home, and stereotypically introverted hobbies such as puzzles and brain teasers.

Dick Clark is a committee legal counsel for the Nebraska Legislature and an attorney in private practice specializing in firearms law. He holds a B.A. in English with minor studies in philosophy from Auburn University. After a stint as librarian at the Ludwig von Mises Institute, he then earned his J.D. from Suffolk Law in Boston. He moved to Nebraska to serve as a policy advisor to Governor Dave Heineman, and later worked at the Platte Institute in Omaha and at the Institute for Economic Inquiry at Creighton University. Dick's second greatest blessing after salvation is his wife Justina, with whom he is raising three children in Lincoln, Nebraska. He serves as a deacon at his Southern Baptist church. Dick enjoys shooting, hunting, playing violin, mandolin, and guitar, and finding time for woodworking in his workshop.

ABOUT THE LIBERTARIAN CHRISTIAN INSTITUTE

The Libertarian Christian Institute is a 501(c)(3) tax-exempt educational and religious nonprofit organization that promotes libertarianism from a Christian point of view. We are convinced that libertarianism is the most consistent expression of Christian political thought. LCI is ecumenical in nature, welcoming all those who confess the traditional creeds of the universal church. LCI originally began as a small website, LibertarianChristians. com, started by Norman Horn in 2008 while he was a graduate student at the University of Texas at Austin. It quickly garnered a loyal following of Christian libertarians and other curious non-Christians, as its emphasis on sound theology and on the concordance of libertarian theory with Christian ethics was not often heard in the libertarian sphere. LCI was incorporated as a nonprofit in 2015 to continue the mission of promoting individual liberty to Christians in a new way.

LCI's goals are to persuade our fellow Christians through online programs, publications, in-person conferences, and regional small group meetups, and to love our fellow libertarians as Jesus would have us do. Our online presence is unmatched in the libertarian community, with hundreds of articles, book reviews, videos, podcasts, news reports, and much more. Our organization is regularly sought after for a Christian libertarian perspective on a variety of political and cultural topics.

As the Libertarian Christian Institute grows, we are actively seeking out donors who desire to see an organization such as this make a positive difference in the church and in the world today for liberty and for Christ. If you would like to participate in our mission to equip the church to make the Christian case for a free society, join us by visiting libertarianchristians.com/donate.

Our Mission: Equip the Church to Promote a Free Society

The Libertarian Christian Institute exists to make the Christian case for a free society and provide the best content to proclaim that libertarianism is the most consistent expression of Christian political thought. We aim to persuade Christians that the political expression of our faith inclines us toward the principles of individual liberty and free markets.

Our Vision: To Create Quality Resources to Equip Christians to Spread the Message of Liberty

We seek to create quality resources to equip Christians to spread the message of liberty in their families, ministries, churches, and among their friends. We view ourselves as a contributor to the vast resources of libertarian content online by making the Christian case for a free society. We resist the assumption that the default political position of Christianity is domination and control, and we combat this by employing studies in history, theology, and biblical exegesis in a variety of venues.

We believe that every Christian libertarian should feel comfortable affirming our Core Values, even if they have their own nuance or "spin" on them. Our aim is not to comprehensively spell out what every Christian libertarian must believe, but provide a central set of tenets that we can all start from, regardless of differences in denomination or theological inclinations.

THE LIBERTARIAN CHRISTIAN INSTITUTE'S CORE VALUES

We believe that every Christian libertarian should feel comfortable affirming our Core Values, even if they have their own nuance or "spin" on them. Our aim is not to comprehensively spell out what every Christian libertarian must believe, but provide a central set of tenets that we can all start from, regardless of differences in denomination or theological inclinations.

1. Christian Political Philosophy Should be Informed by a Holistic View of Scripture, Reason, and Historical Theology

A comprehensive view of the biblical narrative indicates that the Church's proclamation of Jesus' lordship is not a mere personal statement of allegiance; it is also an anti-imperial declaration that the way of peace comes through Christ's counter-cultural kingdom of love and service. Followers of Christ are called to be a prophetic voice against the powers of domination and violence. The State — the monopolized institution of force in society — is never to be confused with the Kingdom of God, and when the power of the state grows, the rightful influence of churches, families, and local communities is diminished.

2. A Free And Civil Society Depends Upon Respect For The Non-Aggression Principle

The ethics modeled by Christ and the early Church call us to change the world and build the Kingdom of God through service rather than force; through persuasion rather than coercion. The use of political force to compel ethical behavior cannot change hearts and only antagonizes our struggle against sin, death, and evil. Christians must call for repentance from sin in humility and never with violence. As such, a consistently Christian ethic always embodies non-aggression.

3. Individual Liberty and the Common Good are not at Odds

As God is intrinsically relational within the Trinity, so also human beings are created to live in community. Sin has marred the communal relationships for which we were created by pitting individuals against God, against one another, and against the earth for which we are called to be wise stewards. Affirming the dignity, worth, and rights of the individual as an image-bearer of God is a first step toward restoring authentic, Christ-centered community among diverse individuals. Because society is comprised of individuals, a healthy society requires healthy individuals. Through voluntary cooperation and respect for freedom, people can join together to trade, innovate, create, collaborate, share, and build a world that simultaneously respects the individual and betters our neighbor.

4. Social Institutions Matter for Human Flourishing

Humans are created to be social beings, and God's design is that we work together to develop institutions which promote human flourishing. Insofar as these institutions are voluntary, peaceful, and non-coercive, human beings possess the God-given capacity to solve the worst of problems in the best of ways. Social institutions founded upon mutual cooperation — such as marriage, family, church, organizations, and businesses — are vital for authentic humanity.

5. Christian Theology Affirms the Essential Tenets of Free Market Economics

Respect for private property, voluntary exchange, condemnation of theft, and the value of cooperation and service towards achieving common goals flow naturally from Christian thought and habit. This is what defines "capitalism" in the libertarian view. Wealth is a tool given by God, and all who possess such wealth are expected to utilize it for God's Kingdom and the good of our neighbor. Taxation and regulation tend to destroy wealth, discourage innovation, and centralize power, and therefore hamper our ability to fulfill the calling of God. Where free markets are allowed to flourish, human beings will prosper both materially and spiritually. Additionally, Christian ethics helps equip our economies for service toward God and neighbor.

Even if you don't call yourself a libertarian, if you share our affinity for these core values, we count you among our ranks. We hope that you will want to partner with us to help spread the message of liberty by making the Christian case for a free society. Help us keep the message alive and growing at underlinelibertarianchristians.com